# NATURE GUIDE TO THE VICTORIA REGION

# Nature Guide
## to the Victoria Region

Edited by Ann Nightingale and Claudia Copley

ROYAL **BC** MUSEUM
PUBLISHING
Victoria, Canada

Published in cooperation with the

VICTORIA NATURAL
HISTORY SOCIETY

Front-cover photograph, "West Coast Presence", by Terry Tuk.
Inside front-cover photograph of Sidney Spit by Darren Copley.
Back-cover photographs by (left, right, top to bottom) Mike Yip, James Miskelly, Derrick Dichburn, Adolf Ceska, Philip Lambert, Marie O'Shaughnessy, Bruce Whittington, Gavin Hanke, Virginia Skilton and Gavin Hanke
Back fold-out photograph of Witty's Lagoon by Pauline Davis.
See page 217 for full credits and copyright information.

Published by the Royal BC Museum, 675 Belleville Street,
    Victoria, British Columbia, V8W 9W2, Canada,
    in association with the Victoria Natural History Society.

Printed in Canada.

The Victoria Natural History Society gratefully acknowledges financial support from VICTORIA FOUNDATION

**Library and Archives Canada Cataloguing in Publication**

Nature guide to the Victoria region / edited by Ann Nightingale and Claudia Copley.

Previously published as: The naturalist's guide to the Victoria region. 1986.
Includes bibliographical references and index.
Copublished by: Victoria Natural History Society.
ISBN 978-0-7726-6575-1

1. Natural history – British Columbia – Victoria Region – Guidebooks.
I. Nightingale, Ann, 1955– II. Copley, Claudia, 1971– III. Victoria Natural History Society (B.C.) IV. Royal BC Museum

QH106.2 B74 N37 2012        508.9711'28        C2012-980152-6

# Contents

Eagle soaring over Tod Inlet.

# Preface

This book is produced by the Victoria Natural History Society as an introduction to the area's natural wonders for residents and visitors. Since 1944, the Society has been providing environmental education through lectures, field trips, checklists and publications. Currently offering at least two field trips every week of the year and four nature-themed presentations each month between September and April, the Victoria Natural History Society has something for both novice and experienced naturalists. It works with other local conservation organizations to preserve habitats, build teaching shelters and viewing platforms, and install interpretive signage at many of the locations mentioned in this guide. Outreach activities include providing naturalists for school field trips and speakers for community events.

Back in 1967, when he was an assistant director at the Provincial Museum of Natural History and Anthropology (now the Royal BC Museum), biologist Yorke Edwards produced the first *Naturalist's Guide to the Victoria Region* as a 38-page booklet identifying interesting places to go and things to see around the capital. He revised the booklet in 1975, and in 1986 developed it into a 200-page book edited by Jim Weston and David Stirling. Now, in 2012, the book has grown to 240 pages, filled with full-colour photographs, completely updated and containing a lot of new information. We have built upon the foundation of the previous versions of the guide, adding new chapters on dragonflies, marine mammals, reptiles and amphibians, nearshore fishes and fungi. This might give you the impression that there is more to see now than there was in 1967. In particular, the bird species on the Victoria region checklist has grown from 246 in the last edition of the guide to more than 380 now. But most of the additions to the species lists come from an increase in reports from people with an interest in their natural environment. While a few newly arrived plants and animals can be found in our area, the reality is that many of our native flora and fauna are under increasing pressure from human activities.

The chapters of this book represent a sampling of popular natural history topics by local experts; they are not exhaustive. The order is alphabetical by topic. We are grateful to the chapter authors: Robert Cannings, Anna Hall, Gavin Hanke, Bryce Kendrick, Philip Lambert, Alan MacLeod, James Miskelly, David Nagorsen, Leon Pavlick and David Stirling, and to the many photographers who have supplied images for this edition. All contributors have donated their works in the spirit of sharing knowledge about our incredible environment. This, in our opinion, is one of the best aspects of the naturalist community – the keen interest of its members in helping others discover special places to observe and conserve our natural environment.

We now have access to technology that wasn't even imagined in 1986, with tools to share our sightings and new discoveries. Online bulletin boards, chat groups and electronic learning resources provide naturalists with constantly updated information on population changes and interesting sightings. Supplemental material to this guide, including recommended readings and up-to-date species checklists will be posted on the Victoria Natural History website (naturevictoria.ca/guide), an option that wasn't even possible for the previous edition of the book.

A book like this does not come together easily. In addition to the authors and photographers, Marie O'Shaughnessy, Bryce Kendrick and Clare Aries contributed many hours to this project. The Victoria Foundation provided early financial support. Another first for us this time around is the publication of our guide by the Royal BC Museum, which brings us full circle in our connection with the museum and its staff, 45 years later. We are most appreciative for the guidance of Gerry Truscott, the museum's publisher, who helped us turn the guide into a more professional and, finally, tangible book.

We hope the *Nature Guide to the Victoria Region* will make your forays into the natural areas of Victoria more interesting and enjoyable. If you are looking for others who share your interests, be sure to check out the Victoria Natural History Society events. And finally, it is our hope that if this guide helps you become more familiar with the natural environment, you will also be compelled to protect what you see and to share what you know.

Ann Nightingale and Claudia Copley

# An Introduction to the Nature of Victoria

## David Stirling

The Victoria region has magnificent scenery, glorious wildflowers and an abundance of terrestrial and marine wildlife. The temperate climate of southern Vancouver Island creates an environment where nature can be enjoyed by residents and visitors throughout the year.

Victoria's climate is markedly different from that of the mainland and most of the rest of Vancouver Island, except for the eastern side north to Nanaimo. We have Washington's spectacular Olympic Mountains and the lower forested Sooke Hills to thank for our Mediterranean climate – damp and mild in winter, warm and dry in summer, rarely hot. There are noticeable microclimates determined by the height of the land, the proximity to the sea, spring cloud cover and the direction of the prevailing winds. These microclimates are important contributors to the region's overall diversity.

The brilliant displays of wildflowers on grassy knolls under Garry Oak and Arbutus trees that are unique to this region of Canada start with the distinctive smell of Indian Plum in bloom. Soon the incomparable blossoms of Satin Flower and Spring Gold appear, followed by Easter Lilies and fields of camas swaying in the wind. In the lowlands and marshes of the region the golden lanterns of Skunk Cabbage provide further hints of spring. By May the Pacific Dogwood, British Columbia's provincial flower, is in full bloom along forest edges. Waves of Oceanspray rolling over hills and roadsides mark Canada Day. The fall and winter also have plenty to offer. October is the time to find masses of Gumweed, Sand Verbena and Mace-head Sedge above the tideline on Victoria's beaches. In November the forest floor produces a riot of colourful fungi, easily rivalling the wildflowers of spring in variety and beauty.

Watching birds is arguably the top outdoor activity for resident and visiting naturalists. An average of 140 bird species have been recorded on recent Christmas bird counts, among the highest in all of Canada. And the birding in the Victoria area is excellent year round. The Victoria Natural History Society's bird checklist names more than 380 species, including 18 gulls. "Follow the birds to Victoria" was the tourist bureau's slogan in the old days, when food scraps were tossed over the stern of the ferries. Gulls no longer follow the ferries in significant numbers, but if you want to identify and separate gull species you will be delighted by a visit to Goldstream Provincial Park in the fall. This is also the time and place for spotting American Dippers and Bald Eagles, and for seeing – and smelling – the results of the salmon spawning spectacle. Waterfowl from all over the province overwinter on our ice-free waterways, and we also have some specialties that birders from around the globe come to see.

Victoria's shores contain many diverse habitats, such as rocky headlands, sandy beaches, kelp beds and mud flats. Inshore waters teem with a stunning variety of marine creatures. On a low tide naturalists can easily appreciate why the diving in our region is considered among the best in the world. The diversity of shrimp, fish, nudibranchs, anemones, mussels, crabs, sea stars, algae and whelks that can be found in a tide pool testifies to the rich coastal water upwelling that helps to maintain this incredible ecosystem. Look out to sea occasionally while exploring the shoreline and you might even see a marine mammal cruising by.

As is often the case with islands, there are fewer species of land mammals in this region than on the mainland. Black-tailed Deer have become common suburban animals, and Raccoons have also adapted well to city life. Watch for playful River Otters and sleek Minks along the shores. Two species of rabbits, both introduced, are regularly seen in the region's green spaces, and the non-native Eastern Grey Squirrel is ubiquitous. Cougars and Black Bears are abundant on Vancouver Island, but encountering one in the Victoria region is only a remote possibility.

Reptiles and amphibians are not numerous in our area, so are a particular pleasure to see. There are no venomous species, and even the protective toxin in the skin of the Rough-skinned Newt is less poisonous on Vancouver Island than in the rest of North America. Garter snakes, which suffer greatly from playful cats and the blades of lawnmowers, are the most often seen reptiles, while the rare and elusive Sharp-tailed Snake prefers steep slopes with difficult access. Two native and two introduced frog species, a toad and several kinds of salamanders also live here. Exotic lizards and turtles abandoned by their owners are becoming established, and in some places they are more numerous than the natives. The Pacific Chorus Frogs singing from ephemeral rainwater ponds and deeper bodies of water call so loudly in March and April that they can drown out traffic noise, but they can still be surprisingly difficult to find.

The Victoria region is noteworthy for many things, but one of the most delightful for naturalists who have spent time in the boreal forest and the Arctic is the absence of biting insects. Nevertheless, we do have some interesting insects, including an amazing array of dragonflies and butterflies. When the birding slows down in the hottest part of the day, don't put your binoculars away, just look at these winged treasures instead. More than

Village Island Reserve, Becher Bay.

60 species of butterflies and almost 50 species of dragonflies have been recorded in the Victoria area, and some species are very common. The Victoria Natural History Society's Butterfly Count, held in the middle of each month from April to September, is a way for naturalists to be involved in local butterfly conservation activities.

Many of the region's parks protect hilltops – Mount Tolmie, Mount Douglas, Observatory Hill and Christmas Hill, to name a few. From these and other summits you will experience spectacular panoramic views of land, sea and sky. Victoria's location, natural beauty and climate have made it a favoured place to live. But more people require more houses, more shopping malls, more parking lots and so on. *More* space for people often translates means *less* habitat for wildlife. To preserve this beautiful place to live, it's important to learn about the plants and animals of the area and to share what we know.

The Victoria Natural History Society has been bringing people to nature and nature to people since 1944. Every month of the year, the Society offers more than a dozen field trips, and each month from September to April it hosts four natural-history presentations. If you prefer company and assistance from a knowledgeable leader, you are welcome to join a group of fellow naturalists on a Victoria Natural History Society field trip.

Why not take the *Nature Guide to the Victoria Region* and strike out to see what you can find? The best time to enjoy the nature of Victoria is right now!

Contact us at:
Victoria Natural History Society
PO Box 24061
Victoria, British Columbia
V8Z 7E7

Website and event calendar: naturevictoria.ca

# Birds

## David Stirling
## Revised and updated by Alan MacLeod

*A quarter century has passed since David Stirling first delivered his advice on birding in the Greater Victoria area. Much has changed in that time and much of the change has had negative impact on our bird populations. Urban developers continue to lay waste to prime bird habitat in our area. Many species David marked as seasonally easy-to-find 26 years ago are much less common now – Western Grebe, Common Tern, Sooty Grouse, Band-tailed Pigeon, Vaux's Swift, Black Swift and Common Nighthawk, to name a few. Some species have all but disappeared – Western Screech-Owl and Western Bluebird come to mind. On the bright side, a small number of species – Trumpeter Swan, Bald Eagle, Barred Owl, Anna's Hummingbird – seem to be coping well enough with human incursion and are more populous in our area than they were in the late 1980s. Who knows what changes will unfold in another quarter century. –* Alan MacLeod

Bald Eagle.

Though the Victoria region is relatively small, it has a great diversity of habitats. Together with its moderate climate, this diversity has given resident and visiting birders a year-round wealth of birds. The Victoria Natural History Society bird checklist indicates more than 370 species seen in our area. Numbers of these are rare visitors (accidentals and vagrants), but some 250 species are seen every year.

Spring comes early in Victoria yet there is no sudden rush of spring migrants. Tree and Violet-green Swallows appear late in February or early March. Soon thereafter, flocks of Brant geese arrive, feeding along suitable shoreline habitats such as Esquimalt Lagoon and Island View Beach. Rufous Hummingbirds appear with the first flowering of Broadleaf Maples and Yellow-rumped Warblers hawk for insects along the margins of Blenkinsop, Swan and Thetis lakes. When later migrants such as Common Nighthawks and Willow Flycatchers arrive at the end of May the resident robins, wrens and towhees have already fledged young. Early May is the time when the largest number of species can be found in the region. Birding enthusiasts have managed to find as many as 135 or more species in the Victoria checklist area in a single day.

Summer is generally a quiet time, especially for woodland birds, but on the islands off Oak Bay, Pelagic Cormorants, Glaucous-winged Gulls and Pigeon Guillemots are at their nesting peak. By mid July the first shorebirds return from the Arctic on their southbound migration. A few young Marbled Murrelets gather from Ogden Point to Cattle Point, Heermann's Gulls arrive after their breeding season far to the south and flocks of Red-necked Phalaropes gather offshore. Fall brings large concentrations of Brandt's

Pelagic Cormorants.

Young Peregrine Falcons.

Cormorants to the Chain Islets from their sea-stack nesting sites on the Washington coast. Turkey Vultures assemble in the Sooke Hills and on the southern tip of Vancouver Island before departing for their southbound journey in late September. Vaux's Swifts gather in smaller numbers in the Metchosin area at the same time. Fall is the season when birders' interest is piqued by the prospect of rarities.

In Canada, only the Vancouver area can compete with Victoria for numbers of winter species. Christmas Bird Counts here consistently register more than 140 species and sometimes exceed 150. In winter, bays and inlets attract large numbers of waterfowl, and the Martindale Flats area is alive with freshwater ducks, which in turn attract raptors, including Peregrine Falcons and rarely even a Gyrfalcon. More than once, fortunate birders have enjoyed a falcon "grand slam" at Martindale, seeing a Peregrine Falcon, Merlin, American Kestrel and Gyrfalcon all on the same day.

You can obtain a copy of the Victoria Natural History Society's *Checklist of Birds* from the VNHS website (see page 12) or a local wild bird store or nature centre. Call the Victoria Natural History Society's Rare Bird Alert at 250-704-2555 for a recorded account of the noteworthy birds in the area. Take a good map with you. The birder's best option is the Davenport *Visitor Guide and Street Guide of Greater Victoria & West Shore*, available in many bookstores. Useful trail maps for the Capital Regional District parks mentioned here – East Sooke, Elk-Beaver Lakes, Francis-King, Horth Hill, Island View Beach, Matheson Lake, Mount Wells, Thetis Lake and Witty's Lagoon – are available online at www.crd.bc.ca/parks/map.htm.

# Birding from the Ferries

Five ferry routes lead to southern Vancouver Island and Victoria. The two shortest and most heavily travelled runs are mentioned here. They both offer good opportunities to enjoy some dramatic birding at the right time of year, while providing birders with an elevated observation post while cruising through inshore and deep-water zones. A word to the wise, however: even in warm weather the speed of the ferries creates a chilly breeze. When you leave the car deck bring a windbreaker along with your binoculars if you plan to be out on the upper decks.

The Port Angeles-Victoria route is served by the MV *Coho*, operated by Black Ball Transport. The crossing time is one hour and 35 minutes. This route may not be as lucrative as the Vancouver-Victoria run, but several species rare or absent in the Strait of Georgia may be seen on the Juan de Fuca crossing. Midsummer is the least productive, fall and winter are good, and the late spring months of March, April and May are usually the best of all.

Leaving Victoria's Inner Harbour and shoreline, look for Common, Pacific and Red-throated loons, Double-crested and Pelagic cormorants, Western, Red-necked and Horned grebes, White-winged and Surf scoters, other duck species, Brant geese (in April), Black Oystercatchers, and Surfbirds.

On Juan de Fuca Strait, Common Murres are numerous, Marbled Murrelets less so, and Rhinoceros Auklets are common from April to October. Ancient Murrelets can be seen there frequently in late fall and early winter. Sometimes large flocks of Bonaparte's Gulls are present in late fall

Common Loon.

and winter. Watch for Red Phalaropes in November and December, the occasional Cassin's Auklets from September to April, and Heermann's Gulls and Parasitic Jaegers in late summer and early fall. Sooty Shearwaters sometimes appear in considerable numbers in Juan de Fuca Strait in fall. Flights of Brant and Surf Scoters are a feature sight in April as they move north from the lagoons of Baja California, and migrating Turkey Vultures may be seen as they fly southward in mid-to-late September.

Waterfowl of several species are most abundant close to the harbour at Port Angeles, which is protected by a narrow spit. Watch for Western Gulls in that area. The amenities of Port Angeles are within walking distance of the ferry terminal so there is no need to bring a vehicle if you intend to re-turn to Victoria on the next sailing.

The Tsawwassen-Swartz Bay ferry route connects Vancouver and Vic-toria via the large vessels of BC Ferries. The voyage usually takes one hour and 40 minutes, sometimes a bit less, and is the best route for birders. Ample parking is provided at both terminals, enabling you to board as a foot passenger for an inexpensive round trip. Seniors in British Columbia can ride free from Monday to Thursday, except on holidays.

As on the Port Angeles run, bird numbers and species vary with the seasons, time of day, weather, tides and the abundance of food, including herring and other sea life. Late May to August is the slack season with only small numbers of locally breeding species: Glaucous-winged Gull, Pelagic and Double-crested cormorants, Black Oystercatcher, Pigeon Guillemot, Marbled Murrelet, Rhinoceros Auklet and Bald Eagle. Action picks up in late August with the arrival of Bonaparte's Gulls and occasional groups of

Pigeon Guillemot.

Red-necked Phalaropes. This is the season to look for Parasitic Jaegers, but be aware that those distant dark birds harassing the Bonaparte's Gulls are more likely to be Heermann's Gulls.

Winter brings huge feeding flocks of Brandt's Cormorants, rafts of Pacific Loons and numerous Bald Eagles. This is the time for big flights of Common Murres, occasional appearances of Ancient Murrelets, and the usual wintering waterfowl such as Common Loons, scoters, goldeneyes, Long-tailed Ducks and Red-breasted Mergansers. Perhaps the best season is spring, from late February to late May, when the herring move inshore to spawn and draw in the birds with them. Your best time for ferry birding is in the morning when the tide is low or starting to flood.

Most of the activity takes place in Active Pass, between Mayne and Galiano islands, and on the approaches to either end of this deep, narrow channel, so make your visit to the cafeteria while the ship is on the less productive stretch of water between the pass and Tsawwassen terminal. Active Pass can produce a bird extravaganza, especially in spring. A passage in March can deliver dozens of Bald Eagles and hundreds of Brandt's Cormorants in addition to Pacific Loons, numerous gulls, Common Murres, scoters, Common Loons, Red-breasted Mergansers and Marbled Murrelets. Eagles crowd the treetops on either side of this channel. Bonuses at this time of year include superb vistas and the sight of Harbour Seals and California Sea Lions. At the westernmost point of Mayne Island, you may even see Killer Whales and porpoises. If you're a visitor looking for your first Northwestern Crow, watch for them as they board the ferry on its arrival at Swartz Bay.

## Other Offshore Opportunities

Weather permitting, mini-pelagic trips can be made to the Chain Islets, out into Juan de Fuca Strait and as far as Race Rocks for species not usually or only distantly seen from shore. These include alcids, shearwaters, storm-petrels and phalaropes. Although the best times are summer and fall, a trip at any time of year in an inflatable Zodiac or similar small craft is always an adventure on the waters off Victoria. It is not only a fine way to observe seabirds but also provides opportunities for seeing exciting marine mammals. Several whale-watching companies operate in Victoria, giving birders a good chance of watching seabirds when cetaceans are not commanding the view.

In summer the Chain Islets feature nesting Pelagic and Double-crested cormorants, Glaucous-winged Gulls and Pigeon Guillemots. In fall, flocks of Red-necked Phalaropes regularly appear, and sometimes you can catch sight of a Wandering Tattler or two on rocky shores. These islets and the Trial Islands are places where many shorebirds sit out high tide. Great Blue Herons seek quiet roosting sites in the Douglas-firs of Discovery Island –

Common Murre.

which features a provincial park – and Chatham Island, which are home to a pair or two of Bald Eagles. These islands are good locations to land, stretch your legs, and look for small woodland birds that may be present in large numbers and good variety in autumn. In winter the area hosts impressive numbers of waterbirds.

The Chain Islets are one of British Columbia's precious Ecological Reserves. Visitors must refrain from disturbing wildlife either by landing on the rocks or by boating too close to nesting birds.

In the fall the waters between Albert Head and Race Rocks and farther south to Constance Bank are often the scene of large concentrations of birds. A prevalent species is the Bonaparte's Gull, which may appear in the thousands. With the gulls there may be alcids, shearwaters, phalaropes and jaegers. Plumes of Glaucous-winged Gulls behind fishing boats on the horizon are signs of good birding to come. The closest launching points from which to explore these waters are at Pedder Bay and Becher Bay, which themselves are good places for water birds.

A caution: Do not venture upon the sea, even for a short trip, without knowledge of tides and weather. If you have little experience on the ocean, take advantage of the skills and equipment of a commercial guide who has both boating and birding expertise. There are very strong rip tides in the channels between the islands, fog can sweep in without warning, and even moderate waves or the wake of a distant ship may swamp a small open boat. Even if it's a warm day on land, wear wool or synthetic-pile clothing to keep you warm under waterproof pants and jacket. Protect your binoculars, camera and lunches from salt spray and splashes by using plastic bags or cases designed for marine conditions. Rubber boots are your best choice for stepping between small boats and the shore.

Hooded Mergansers.

# Field Stops for Birding

A recommended Victoria birding tour is described below, including selected field stops and the birds you might see during various times of year. The entire route, with the exception of East Sooke and Matheson Lake parks in the western portion of the region, can be covered in one day, although more time spent observing brings more rewards. Those two parks require at least a day, and of course are worth many visits. Begin this tour in Beacon Hill Park at the southern extremity of Victoria.

Goodacre Lake and the other park ponds attract a variety of waterfowl, especially in winter. Eurasian Wigeons, the Greater and Lesser scaups and Hooded Mergansers are among the regulars, but other species – including Northern Pintail, Wood Duck and Gadwall – sometimes show up. Check the model yacht pond beside Dallas Road near its junction with Government Street for ducks and gulls. Though much less conspicuous than in former years, introduced California Quail are sometimes still seen in thickets from Beacon Hill to the Dallas Road cliffs. The park's wooded areas and thickets shelter a good variety of the region's songbirds and sometimes turn up a rarer prize too. In late summer and fall shoreline rocks and beaches along Dallas Road harbour Surfbirds, Black Turnstones, Sanderlings, Dunlins and the occasional Rock Sandpiper or Wandering Tattler. From October to May many kinds of waterfowl congregate here. Lover's Lane in the southeast corner of the park, at the junction of Cook Street and Dallas Road, is a small oasis of woodland habitat attracting warblers and other songbird migrants in spring and fall – and sometimes Barred or Great Horned owls.

Clover Point, a half-kilometre east of the park, is not what it was three decades ago, but it remains a good place to look for waterfowl, shorebirds and gulls – including the kinds of rarities that get birders all aquiver. Harlequin Ducks are found here year-round. In fall Lapland Longspurs and Snow Buntings regularly appear and, from time to time in winter, a lucky birder has found a Snowy Owl parked on one of the point's lamp standards. As often as not, when something special turns up in our area – Little Gull,

Osprey at its nest. The wasps are attracted to the fish it's captured.

Sabine's Gull, Cassin's Auklet, Northern Fulmar, Ruff, Sharp-tailed Sandpiper, you name it – it is seen from Clover Point. The entire area from Clover Point to Ogden Point, three kilometres westward, merits close attention. A winter to early-spring walk from Beacon Hill to Clover Point and then to Ogden Point can readily deliver an observant birder fifty species or more.

The entire Oak Bay waterfront from Gonzales Bay to Cattle Point is good for birding, particularly in winter. Summer features Pelagic Cormorants, Pigeon Guillemots and Marbled Murrelets. Late summer and fall bring many shorebirds. At the old Chinese Cemetery at Harling Point watch for Harlequin Ducks, Black Oystercatchers, and Black Turnstones. The cemetery site was selected for its excellent *feng shui* (literally 'wind-water' in Chinese) and marks an auspicious geographic location. The famous flower gardens of Victoria and the superb views of sea and mountains dominated by distant Mount Baker are added attractions as you make your way north along the Oak Bay shoreline. At Cattle Point you will find ample parking, two boat launching ramps and plenty of room for a picnic. Harlequin Ducks are found here, oystercatchers are common, and the tidal currents attract alcids and sea ducks. Though a notch or two behind Clover Point, Cattle Point is another excellent spot for rarities. The Garry Oak forests of nearby Uplands Park, extending westward behind the point, support populations of the area's common breeding landbirds.

Ten Mile Point provides a good chance to see alcids such as Marbled and Ancient murrelets, for the headland here places you closer to seabirds moving between Juan de Fuca Strait, Puget Sound and the Strait of

21

Western Tanager.

Georgia. In spring and fall the trees nearby are a gathering area for migrating songbirds.

Though its natural areas are diminishing, the University of Victoria campus still offers good birding. In May a generous assortment of breeding songbird species in wooded areas and gardens may include less common species such as Black-headed Grosbeak and Hutton's Vireo. The university woods are likely the best near-downtown location to find Hairy Woodpecker; other woodpecker species like the habitat here too. Barred and Great Horned owls are reliable nighttime denizens of the university's woods. A good spot to look for all these is a wide pathway leading north from Cedar Hill Cross Road, just a hundred metres or so east of University Drive. Check the woods to your left and the ravine to your right as you enter the pathway. The wooded areas are laced with footpaths affording access to good habitat.

Less than a kilometre west along Cedar Hill Cross Road is the entrance to Mount Tolmie Park. Aside from the attractions of its Garry Oak meadows, carpets of wildflowers and the excellent hilltop views over the city, Mount Tolmie is a magnet for migrating passerines in both spring and fall. Mountain Bluebirds in April and Lazuli Buntings and Ash-throated Flycatchers in May are just some of the specialties that annually attract birders to Mount Tolmie.

A stop in Mount Douglas Park may reward a birder with a good assortment of regularly occurring landbirds. It is also an excellent area to look for warblers and other passerine migrants in spring, notably Western Tanagers. Instead of driving to the summit parking lot, walk the paths in the southside forest. One of several good access points is by way of a marked footpath beside Blenkinsop Road just south of Lohbrunner Road. The path leads through attractive, open Garry Oak habitat, eventually leading to "Little Mount Doug" in the shadow of the main peak. This is an excellent spot to rest in May, watch the world go by and wait for something good to fly overhead or land on a nearby treetop.

On the opposite side of Mount Douglas Park from Blenkinsop Road, Cordova Bay Road leads to a large picnic area parking lot overlooking the seaside bluffs on the northeast side of the park. There is easy access here to the gravel beach where rafts of waterfowl winter. This is now the best remaining shoreline location in Victoria to look for Eared Grebe.

Northern Pintail.

Back on Blenkinsop Road, Blenkinsop Lake can be reached by turning west onto Lohbrunner Road. Walk Lochside Trail to the Victoria Natural History Society's observation platform and the handsome pedestrian trestle bridge crossing over the lake. This popular walking and biking path is bird-productive, particularly for songbirds in spring and a good variety of waterfowl in late fall and winter. In spring the thick growth of willows and Red-osier Dogwood along the trail conceals singing Yellow Warblers and Black-headed Grosbeaks. From here, with patience and a little luck, you may spot Wood Ducks or even a Green Heron. Blenkinsop Lake can also be reached via Lochside Trail from the south, where you'll find more ample parking on Cumberland Road via Borden Street and Morris Drive.

King's Pond is a little urban wetland at the north end of Cedar Hill Municipal Golf Course. Access to the pond is by Queensbury Avenue via Blenkinsop Road. Despite the nearby golfers and the pond's popularity with strollers, this little oasis harbours a good number and variety of waterfowl from fall to early spring. Wood Ducks often appear here and sometimes a rarity, such as a Tufted Duck, makes an appearance.

Nearby Swan Lake is another urban wetland that delivers a generous variety of ducks and waterbirds. The Swan Lake environs were the first Chinese Auspicious Feng Shui site in Canada. Birds like it too. A surprising number of rarities appear here despite the park's popularity with walkers. One neighbourhood birder recently tallied 166 species here in a single year. The surrounding woods and the feeding station maintained at the visitor centre attract a good variety of songbirds, especially in spring. While it's not likely you'll hear the entertaining "oonk-a-loonk, oonk-a-loonk" of the American Bittern, Swan Lake is still the most reliable place in our area to find this secretive marsh-loving species. Look for it on a still, sunny day feeding along the edges of Colquitz Creek. A good vantage point is the

Red-tailed Hawk chased by a Cooper's Hawk.

Saanich Municipal Hall helipad overlooking the west-side marshes. The parking lot for Swan Lake can be reached via Rainbow Street and Ralph Street from McKenzie Avenue.

Rithet's Bog (called Shadywood Park on the Davenport map) lies beside Chatterton Way, off Quadra Street just east of the Patricia Bay Highway. This area attracts a variety of freshwater waterfowl in winter and a good array of migrants and breeding species, especially in spring. One on-street parking option is along Dalewood Lane near the north end of Chatterton. A well-maintained footpath leads around the circumference of the bog. The wooded interior of the bog and wooded areas preserved among the suburban developments to the east attract a variety of woodpeckers and forest passerines. A springtime circumnavigation of Rithet's can easily deliver 40 species or more, including those not readily encountered elsewhere, such as Sora and Virginia Rail.

A few kilometres north, accessible by Martindale Road, lies Martindale Flats, still the best Christmas Bird Count zone in all Canada. Like so many other key birding areas in our region, Martindale's vitality as habitat for birds has suffered from human development, but Christmas Bird Count talliers in charge of the Martindale zone are still disappointed if they don't turn up a hundred species every year. The farm fields here provide wintering grounds for a host of freshwater ducks. It is the best place in Victoria for observing raptors in winter. Peregrine Falcons are regularly found here during the cold months, sometimes Gyrfalcons, too, though less frequently in recent years. Rough-legged Hawks, rare on Vancouver Island, occur here more often than anywhere else on the island. Passerine and non-passerine rarities turn up every winter. Martindale Flats and the fields on either side of Island View Road are still favoured habitat of the introduced Sky Lark.

The best times to find them are on sunny days from March to July, when males sing spectacularly over their territories.

Island View Beach is excellent for waterfowl and alcids in winter. Three loon species, as well as Red-necked Grebes and Common Murres are regular. Small numbers of Black Scoters can be found at the northern end of the beach, the most reliable location for this species in greater Victoria. The northern end of the beach draws good passerine migrants in fall – Lapland Longspurs, Snow Buntings and others.

North of the town of Sidney there are several bays and harbours, including Blue Heron Basin and, just beside the final approach to Swartz Bay ferry terminal, Tsehum Slough. Here the mud flats attract shorebirds at low tide. In winter a good variety of waterbirds hang out.

If you're a visitor arriving by air at the Victoria Airport, you're at a good spot for finding a Sky Lark, a prime target species for birders coming to Victoria. In spring, just step outside the terminal building, make your way to the closest chain-link fence with an open view of the runways and listen for the remarkably sustained aerial song of this introduced species. Another good vantage point is at the north end of Canora Road on the eastern side of the airport area. While you're enjoying the Sky Larks keep an eye peeled for other open-country fliers – Northern Harriers, Western Meadowlarks and American Kestrel among them.

Opposite the northwest corner of the airport is productive Patricia Bay, a magnet for big numbers of wintering sea ducks and waterfowl including Barrow's Goldeneye and the occasional Black Scoter. Farther south along the Saanich Inlet shoreline, loons, grebes and bay ducks are often found in the quiet, shallow waters of Coles Bay Regional Park.

Great Blue Heron.

Gadwall.

American Coot.

Our tour now moves south via Highway 17 to Elk Lake Park where a pair of Bald Eagles are likely to be watching the action from the trees across the lake. In winter you will find rafts of waterfowl including Common and Hooded mergansers, big numbers of American Coots, and occasionally Trumpeter Swans and Mute Swans. Canvasbacks and Ruddy Ducks, seldom seen elsewhere in the area, sometimes favour the north end of the lake – and in good numbers too.

South of Elk Lake take Royal Oak Drive west to West Saanich Road, then proceed north to Markham Road. Go west (left) a short distance to a very limited roadside parking area next to a gated path. This leads to the Victoria Natural History Society observation platform at the edge of a shallow pond locals know as Quick's Bottom. This wetland is more choked with vegetation than in years gone by but it can still be productive in winter and spring for several species of ducks, including Gadwall. Blue-winged Teals and an occasional Cinnamon Teal stop by in spring and summer. Marsh Wrens prefer this area while American Bitterns and Solitary Sandpipers are occasionally recorded. Red-tailed Hawks perch in the oak trees at the northeast edge of the pond and patrol their domain for likely hunting prospects.

A well-marked footpath a hundred yards west of the Quick's Bottom pull-out leads through a woodland to fields adjacent to attractive Viaduct Flats, favoured by a variety of waterfowl from fall to early spring. The adjacent woodlands are productive too for migrant and breeding passerines and woodpeckers. On the west side, the flats can also be reached by Interurban Road. Opposite the east end of Viaduct Avenue you will find the Victoria Natural History Society viewing stand and ample parking.

Not far north of Viaduct Flats stands attractive Little Saanich Mountain, reached by West Saanich Road. Early in the last century this hill was selected as the site of a federal astronomical observatory. The observatory

Marsh Wren.

is still active and the hilltop commands terrific views to the south and west. In May Little Saanich Mountain is an excellent place to look for good numbers of passerines, both migrants and returning breeders. You can drive to the top if the gate is unlocked, or you can get there on foot, either by way of the paved road or trails. Mountain Bluebirds sometimes stop by in mid April. Hammond's and Olive-sided flycatchers, House Wrens and Western Tanagers are a few of the rewards your efforts may reap. If you need a rest, look for a beautiful, unusual bench south of the big hilltop observatory. Have a sit and count your blessings while enjoying the bird chorus and your view of a lovely patch of Garry Oak meadow saturated with spring wildflowers.

Make your way to West Burnside Road, then north to Munn's Road and Millstream Road through the Highlands. This route holds less interest in winter but from March to September the birding here is very good. Stop at the power line dividing Francis-King and Thetis Lake parks and explore on foot, especially the right of way running south at the western boundary of Francis-King Park. Many people consider power lines ugly. Songbirds seem to disagree. In May an observant birder can turn up 50 species in this area, including all 8 of the region's breeding warbler species. Turkey Vultures, Cooper's Hawks, Red-tailed Hawks and Bald Eagles are regular, while Golden Eagles visit occasionally. California Quails, Band-tailed Pigeons, Pacific-slope and Willow flycatchers, House Wrens, Swainson's Thrush, Cassin's Vireos, Western Tanagers and Red Crossbills are all likely at the right time of year. Wood Ducks nest in the ponds near the Pike Lake Substation, and if you are lucky, you may catch a glimpse of a Beaver, an uncommon sighting on southern Vancouver Island.

One of the crown jewels in greater Victoria's park system is Gowlland Tod Provincial Park, accessible via Millstream Road in the Highlands. The park is a big one with a network of excellent trails. One of the fastest, most efficient avenues into some of the best areas is by Emma Dickson Trail which starts on the left side of the road just 15 metres or so beyond Emma Dixon Road. The park's western edges feature open Garry Oak-Arbutus forest on high bluffs commanding spectacular views of Finlayson Arm and the Sooke Hills to the west. The park is an excellent birding and hiking destination at any time of year; fall is good but spring, particularly May, is best of all. Gowlland Tod is home to most of the region's breeding songbirds, including several that are more difficult to find elsewhere. Hammond's Flycatchers, House Wrens, Townsend's Solitaires and Red Crossbills are some of the passerines that draw birders here. Raptors are a draw, too: Northern Goshawk, Northern Pygmy-Owl, and even the occasional Golden Eagle. And if the birding is slow, never mind – there is an infinite supply of terrific vistas to distract you.

Return to Millstream Road and head south, then take the Trans-Canada Highway to Goldstream Provincial Park for your best local shot at American Dipper. Stop at the bridge at the campground entrance and scan the river for the dipper, which nests there. From October to March dippers are more readily seen on the river at the picnic site. En route to "Goldstream Flats" at the river estuary look for Red-breasted Sapsuckers. In fall and early winter large numbers of gulls gather to feed on dying salmon. One or two Glaucous Gulls regularly appear among the salmon-eating throngs.

Violet-green Swallow.

If you are in reasonably good physical condition and have an extra half day, hike the steep but well-marked "Mount Finlayson Trail" out of Goldstream Park up to the summit of Mount Finlayson, about a one-hour climb. Mount Finlayson once commanded a spectacular view over the Highlands, but alas, the view is now corrupted by a development immediately south. Still, from the top you may be rewarded with sightings of Turkey Vultures, Bald Eagles, Steller's Jays, and possibly even an occasional Golden Eagle. Watch for Violet-green Swallows

Double-crested Cormorant colony on Mandarte Island.

catching insects wafted up the rock face overlooking Goldstream Flats and the Freeman King Visitor Centre. The summit area is an excellent vantage point from which to watch the aerobatic antics of resident ravens. Keep the city in view on the descent, until you're near the lower woods, or you might stray onto the slippery southwest bluffs. Another trail, steeper and less used, descends the mountain on its northwest side, returning you to the road a short distance north of the regular trailhead.

To continue this tour, take the Trans-Canada Highway back to the exit for Highway 1A, connecting with Jacklin Road and then Metchosin Road to reach Witty's Lagoon Regional Park. Here, and westward over the Sooke Hills, you can expect to see many Turkey Vultures gathering in September, and occasionally numbers of Vaux's Swifts. The woodlands near the water are visited by Hutton's Vireos and by migrating warblers in spring and fall. The mud flats and Witty's Beach attract many shorebirds and ducks, including occasional rarities and strays. Ospreys and Bald Eagles nest in the area. From the regional park take Duke Road to Olympic View Drive, park beside the open field and walk out to rocky Tower Point, where you can usually find grebes, cormorants and other seabirds – and occasionally something special, like a Yellow-billed Loon.

Matheson Lake Park and East Sooke Park are thick with forests covering rugged hills, where woodland birds can be found year-round. Both parks boast good hiking trails that deserve time and repeated visits. Creyke Point, near East Sooke's Aylard Farm, is a good seabird location and commands magnificent views over Becher Bay, Juan de Fuca Strait and Washington's Olympic Mountains. East Sooke is a dependable area for finding Band-tailed Pigeons in fall. A pair of Golden Eagles has nested in this area

Barred Owl.

and this species is regularly seen in fall from the park's principal hawk-watching vantage points, Lookout Hill and Babbington Hill. Water-birds go about their business along East Sooke's rocky shores, notably in fall and winter. Great Horned Owls, Barred Owls, and Northern Pygmy-Owls can be heard in this park. Hutton's Vireos appear in the woods bordering the meadows at Aylard Farm. Turkey Vultures are a common sight on summer days and are often present in the hundreds in late September before the big birds depart south across Juan de Fuca Strait. Lookout Hill rising above Becher Bay is a choice spot for watching them soar and also for admiring the Olympic range across the water.

Mount Wells Regional Park is the most reliable near-Victoria location for finding Sooty Grouse. The park affords a pleasant hike into attractive open Garry Oak-Arbutus habitat and excellent viewpoints in every direction. Of several trail options, the official trailhead to Mount Wells is on Humpback Road, a short distance west of Irwin Road. The trailhead is well marked and ample parking provided. Mount Wells attracts a good variety of migrant and breeding songbirds and is a good raptor-finding spot as well. This is a good location to find early migrating warblers. Band-tailed Pigeons and Northern Pygmy-Owls sometimes show up here. Apart from its birding potential, Mount Wells has much to offer wildflower lovers, too. Vast carpets of beautiful Satinflowers adorn the hilltop ridge in mid March.

Our route back to Victoria is by way of Esquimalt Lagoon where masses of waterfowl are present from October to May. Shorebirds gather here in late summer and fall, and gulls are abundant. Western Meadowlarks and Horned Larks are sometimes sighted in the beach grasses along Coburg Peninsula. Watch the small island near the east end of the lagoon for herons, gulls and shorebirds.

For those with an extra day to explore, a birding trip out along Vancouver Island's southwest coast is highly recommended. From Sooke to Jordan River, Highway 14 follows the shore providing magnificent vistas of the Olympic Mountains and Cape Flattery, the northwesternmost point of Washington. In midsummer the countryside is noticeably greener than around Victoria and is favoured habitat of Varied Thrushes, Steller's Jays and Fox Sparrows. Watch for Bald Eagles and Ospreys near the shore and Turkey Vultures overhead. Whiffin Spit, at the entrance to Sooke Basin, is a worthwhile side-trip to check for migrating shorebirds. Look for Black Scoters and occasional rarities such as Yellow-billed Loon. Out along the spit a less disturbed habitat prevails and groups of Black Oystercatchers probe the gravel beach, often hollering at everyone in sight.

## A Few Words About Gulls

Victoria is a paradise for gulls and gull-watchers. Eighteen species have been recorded here. Of these, seven are regular and common. The Glaucous-winged Gull is the common resident, breeding in large numbers on rocky islets. California Gulls are common in summer, Bonaparte's are abundant migrants, while Mew, Herring and Thayer's gulls are plentiful in winter. Heermann's Gull, a Victoria specialty, is a late summer visitor from the Sea of Cortez in the Gulf of California. Other species range from the once-recorded Ross's Gull to the rare but regular transients, Franklin's Gull, Iceland Gull and Glaucous Gull. Scope out Victoria's sewage outfalls, especially Clover Point, for interesting gulls. Gull identification, particularly when it comes to immature birds, is a challenge even to the birding expert, and the variations within each variety of plumage of the different species and the presence of hybrids adds spice to a day of birding.

Glaucous-winged Gull (left) and Heermann's Gull (above).

# Notes on Some Local Specialties

**Brant**: From March to mid May a common migrant to shores and lagoons. On their spring migration they closely follow the shoreline north from their wintering areas in the lagoons of Baja California to Juan de Fuca Strait and north along both coasts of Vancouver Island. In fall they fly directly across the Gulf of Alaska to the coasts of Washington and Oregon, missing Vancouver Island.

**Mute Swan** and **Trumpeter Swan**: The introduced Mute Swan is common at Esquimalt Lagoon, the Gorge Inlet and small lakes. Trumpeter Swans are increasingly common winter visitors to Martindale Flats, Tod Creek Flats and other rain-flooded areas.

**Wood Duck**: King's Pond is usually the most reliable site near the urban core. The ponds just east of the Pike Lake Substation at Munn's Road are also fairly dependable.

**Canvasback**: Not always a sure bet in our area. Portage Inlet and the north end of Elk Lake are most dependable.

**Black Scoter**: The north end of Island Beach, toward Cordova Spit, and Patricia Bay in North Saanich.

**Eurasian Wigeon**: An uncommon but regular winter visitor to Beacon Hill Park, King's Pond, Martindale Flats and other watery places. Handsomer than his North American cousin, the drake is always easy to pick out of the largest gangs of American Wigeons.

**Harlequin Duck**: This outlandishly decked-out resident favours the rocky shores of Clover Point, Harling Point and Cattle Point. Common and easy to find in winter.

A Trumpeter Swan chasing off a Mute Swan.

**Ruddy Duck**: Seen at the north end of Elk Lake in winter.

**Sooty Grouse**: Much less prevalent close to Victoria than in years gone by. Prospects improve as you head west. Mount Wells in Metchosin is reliable, as are the Sooke Hills farther west. This grouse typically refuses to show itself even as the male sounds his territorial serenade.

**California Quail**: Introduced and declining, particularly in urban areas. Still fairly common in brushy, less-travelled locations. Listen for its charming, quirky territorial call: "*where-are-you? where-are-you?*"

Harlequin Duck.

**Red-throated Loon**: Less numerous than its Common and Pacific cousins. Esquimalt Lagoon is a good bet.

**Western Grebe**: Declining in waters next to the urban core. Royal Roads University at Esquimalt Lagoon is perhaps the best remaining locale.

**Eared Grebe**: Look for this bird at Mount Douglas Beach in winter. Leave your car in the parking lot at Cedar Hill and Cordova Bay roads, and walk down to the beach.

Wood Ducks are increasing in numbers in this area.

Left: Bald Eagle and nestlings.

Facing page: Black Oystercatcher (above) and Black Turnstones.

**Shearwaters** and **petrels**: Typically rare but possible from August to December off Clover Point and Cadboro (Ten Mile) Point. Boat trips into Juan de Fuca Strait may be productive. Shearwaters occasionally turn up in larger numbers in later summer. The most likely species are Sooty Shearwater and Fork-tailed Storm Petrel from August to October. Short-tailed Shearwaters may be present in the strait in winter months.

**Brandt's Cormorant** and **Pelagic Cormorant**: Brandt's is common on the Chain Islets from August to March with fewer numbers roosting on rocks along the Victoria shore. Big flocks fly past Clover Point and a few non-breeders loiter around the Victoria waterfront all summer. The Pelagic Cormorant is a common resident on rocky shores.

**Bald Eagle**: Easy to find in winter but less numerous in summer, this big eagle nests at a few points along our shores. Its population builds in winter and during March when herring spawn. In spring Active Pass is the best place to see Bald Eagles in numbers, and in late fall Goldstream estuary is their site of choice during the salmon die-off.

**Falcons**: Peregrines are regular winter visitors to Martindale Flats and are quite often seen bulleting past Clover Point, but they can be seen occasionally almost anywhere, even from urban vantage points. Keep an eye skyward. Gyrfalcons rarely turn up at Martindale Flats, especially in recent years. Keep an eye cocked skyward for Merlins anywhere in the region. American Kestrels are most often encountered on or near the Victoria Airport.

**Black Oystercatcher**: This raucous, common resident can be found at low tide almost anywhere along Victoria's shores.

**Wandering Tattler**: Uncommon but regular on rocky coasts, this shorebird appears in ones or twos from late April to mid May and again from mid July to mid September. Good localities include Ogden Point, the headlands of the Oak Bay Golf Course and shores west of Sooke.

Usually solitary, this bird often escapes notice as it feeds in rocky gutters and crevices close to the breaking surf.

**Black Turnstone**: This charmer is an abundant visitor to all our shores, from late summer to late spring.

**Surfbird**: Can be seen in migration during May, August and September. Small numbers overwinter and regularly occur along the shore anywhere from Ogden Point to Cattle Point.

**Rock Sandpiper**: The last winter resident to arrive on the shores of the Victoria region. It is scarce, seen alone or in small parties on the rocks or beaches from Ogden Point to Cattle Point, November to late April.

**Red Phalarope**: An uncommon late-fall, early-winter migrant to Juan de Fuca Strait, this species is occasionally found inshore along the westerly beaches of our area, but you're far better situated for close viewing aboard a boat.

Band-tailed Pigeon (right) and
Anna's Hummingbird (above).

**Parasitic Jaeger**: An uncommon late summer and fall migrant, this pirate can sometimes be seen harrying Common Terns and Bonaparte's Gulls off Oak Bay, Esquimalt Lagoon, Pedder Bay and Becher Bay.

**Heermann's Gull**: This gull reverses the normal practice, indulging in a northward post-breeding dispersal. Fairly common on rocks and beaches all the way from Jordan River to Island View Beach from late July to October. Occasionally one lingers into winter.

**Thayer's Gull**: Common from September to April along our shores. The Goldstream River in winter is a good spot to find Thayer's and other gulls attracted by the remains of spawned-out salmon. Sometimes it appears in fair numbers at Clover Point and in much greater numbers on islets such as Race Rocks.

**Western Gull**: Preferring the outer (west) coast of Vancouver Island, this gull is a rare winter visitor to Victoria's shores, but can sometimes show up at Clover Point. Pure Western Gulls are much scarcer than Western × Glaucous-winged hybrids.

**Pigeon Guillemot**: A common resident of inshore waters, this bird nests in crevices and under drift logs on the Chain Islets and, more conveniently for birders, on the wharf opposite the Ogden Point breakwater.

**Marbled Murrelet**: Declining in our area, this bird can usually be found in pairs or family groups of threes. It has a habit of tipping up and diving when approached, earning it the endearing fisherman's moniker "Kissmearse".

**Ancient Murrelet**: A late-fall and winter visitor in variable numbers, it can be spotted from Clover and Cadboro points, and around the Chain Islets. Best located by an application of patience and a good spotting scope.

**Rhinoceros Auklet**: A common summer visitor, scarcer but regular at other times of year. The area from Ogden Point to Clover Point is reliable.

**Band-tailed Pigeon**: Encountered much less frequently than in the past. Found in both coniferous and oak forests, it is usually silent and sits tight in foliage. Likes to feed on acorns. Depending on the winter supply of these and the non-native English Holly berries, the pigeons may be a little more numerous in some winters.

Red-breasted Sapsucker.

**Western Screech Owl**: Much declined in our area, perhaps partly due to depredations by the insurgent Barred Owl. Now, infrequent sightings – or soundings – are usually reported on the Victoria Natural History Society's Rare Bird Alert: 250-704-2555.

**Black Swift**: Declining in our area, and now uncommon to rare from mid May to September, when it appears in small flocks ahead of storm fronts. More likely to be seen north of the Malahat.

**Vaux's Swift**: Declining and uncommon from May to September at Goldstream Provincial Park and in the Metchosin area, where it assembles in September before leaving for warmer southern climes.

**Anna's Hummingbird**: A great success story – this tiny bird has colonized the Victoria area, and is now a thriving, common resident sustained in winter by the softheartedness of people with feeders.

**Red-breasted Sapsucker**: An uncommon winter visitor to Goldstream Provincial Park, this species is regular in the Western Hemlock forests west of Sooke and frequently seen on the grounds of Royal Roads University. During cold snaps in winter it is given to abandoning its usual haunts and turning up in urban areas, sometimes in large numbers. One good spot is the line of Scots Pines extending north of Lover's Lane in Beacon Hill Park. This woodpecker is common in spring north of the Malahat in mixed hemlock and maple woodlands.

**Hammond's Flycatcher**: Uncommon and mostly observed on its spring migration. It breeds at higher elevations in the Victoria region. Gowlland Tod Provincial Park, Little Saanich Mountain and Spectacle Lake Provincial Park on the Malahat are good bets.

**Pacific-slope Flycatcher**: This summer visitor to middle elevations of mixed woods is more likely to be found at lower elevations than Hammond's Flycatcher.

**Sky Lark**: An uncommon, introduced local resident, the Sky Lark frequents large fields on the Saanich Peninsula. Only three reliable areas are left: the Victoria International Airport, the fields adjacent to Martindale Road and Island View Road, and – the best location – the farm fields between Wallace Drive and Central Saanich Road north of Straits View. The best time to see it is in the early morning and on sunny, calm days from March to July, when this storied songbird sings as it flies in wide circles overhead.

**Steller's Jay**: A resident of forested areas west and north of the urban core. The population of British Columbia's noisy provincial bird fluctuates considerably – it's common throughout the area in some years and scarce in others.

**Northwestern Crow**: The only crow you will see in Victoria – and you'll see it a lot. Sometimes aggressive near the nest in breeding season, and in winter its vacant nests are apparent in trees throughout Victoria. This species delivers one of the area's great bird spectacles on late fall and winter afternoons: huge flocks fly northward across Cordova Bay en route to roosting sites on several small Gulf Islands.

**Chestnut-backed Chickadee**: No other species of chickadee is found in our area, but this one is a common resident throughout the region.

**Bushtit**: Common in brushy areas where it moves about in flocks. Attractive, charming, confiding and trusting, the bushtit's delicately woven hanging nest is often encountered at or just above eye-level in a variety of trees and bushes, sometimes right over the sidewalk.

**American Dipper**: A small population of these entertaining little birds maintains itself at Goldstream Provincial Park. Watch for it as it dives below the surface of the Goldstream River and walks about in search of food. In summer it frequents the section between the picnic-area bridge and Freeman King Visitor Centre, and in winter look in the vicinity of the campground bridge. The observant visitor to other creeks and rivers west of Victoria may spot dippers, usually in winter.

**Bewick's Wren**: This common resident of brushy forest edges and suburban gardens is one of our most tireless and versatile songsters.

**Western Bluebird**: Once a breeding species in Metchosin and on Saltspring Island, this attractive bird is now encountered only as a sporadic wayfarer. Count yourself lucky if you happen to see one.

Steller's Jay.

Varied Thrush.

**Varied Thrush**: Its range in Canada is almost exclusively in British Columbia and the Yukon. Near Victoria it is evident in winter but best seen
year-round in Goldstream Provincial Park. Listen for its distinctive call
in heavy forest: Bear Hill Regional Park, Mount Douglas Park, Thetis
Lake Regional Park, particularly its northern sections (Scafe Hill and
Stewart Mountain), and in coniferous forests west of Sooke. During
cold snaps in winter this species often moves into city parks such as
Beacon Hill.

**Hutton's Vireo**: A quiet, secretive, uncommon resident, best located in
spring by its loud, distinctive *zweep* call. Good locations are the University of Victoria's woods and nearby Mystic Ravine and in the woodland
between Quick's Bottom and Viaduct Flats.

**Black-throated Grey Warbler**: Best located by song, which is similar to
Townsend's Warbler but distinctly buzzier, this warbler is not as common as Townsend's but is easy enough to find in breeding season on dry
mixed-wooded hillsides at Munn's Road, Viaduct Flats, Little Saanich
Mountain and Horth Hill Regional Park in North Saanich.

**Townsend's Warbler**: Common from April to August in the canopy of
tall coniferous forests. Good locations are Francis-King Regional Park,
Munn's Road, Thetis Lake Regional Park and Gowlland Tod Provincial
Park.

**Golden-crowned Sparrow**: Small gangs winter in thickets and hedgerows, often in the vicinity of bird feeders. In late April and early May a
large migration passes through Victoria.

**House Finch**: An abundant resident in city gardens, weedy fields and
hedgerows.

# Butterflies

## James Miskelly

In 1884, George Taylor wrote on the subject of Victoria's insect fauna:

> *The extreme abundance of butterflies cannot fail to strike an observer. Nearly 40 species may be marked abundant. A patch of blossom in May, covered with blues and fritillaries, with an occasional sulphur and two or three magnificent species of swallowtail is a sight such as the British naturalist, at least, never sees at home. Later in the year hundreds of ladies, coppers, skippers, and admirals make a different, but no less pleasing, picture.*

At that time, Victoria was known for its butterflies, and naturalists came from across North America to see them. One naturalist visiting from New York recorded 50 species in the Victoria area in the years 1892 and 1893. On his annotated list, the word "common" appears beside 33 species. Today, these observations could not be repeated. But the mild, semi-Mediterranean climate and diverse plant communities of Victoria still support a richness of butterflies unexpected in coastal British Columbia. Taking the time to learn about and seek out our butterfly fauna well repays the effort.

Sixty-one butterfly species have been recorded in the Victoria area. These include seven migratory species, three that have become established here through human activities, and fifty-one native residents. Unfortunately, many species historically found in the Victoria area are not seen here anymore. These include truly rare and endangered species, such as Taylor's Checkerspot and the Island Blue, as well as species that have disappeared from our area inexplicably, while remaining common elsewhere in British Columbia, such as the Dreamy Duskywing and Roadside Skipper. Today, a well-prepared observer who knows how and where to look could expect to see 30 to 35 butterfly species in a year, without leaving greater Victoria.

# Enjoying Butterflies

## How to Find Them

The best way to find butterflies is to know a little bit about them. All butterflies have four distinct stages in their life cycles: egg, larva (caterpillar), pupa (chrysalis) and adult. Each of these stages has its own requirements for life. When searching for butterflies, the most important life stages to know about are the larva and the adult. The larva feeds on vegetation and can be very particular about which plants it will eat. These plants, which biologists call "host" plants, define the breeding habitat, and the adults are usually found close by. Adult butterflies feed on flower nectar, wet earth, rotten fruit, sap and any other liquids that contain dissolved nutrients. They are almost invariably creatures of bright sunshine. So, the best places to find adult butterflies are sunny areas near the larval host plants where there is an abundance of nectar-producing flowers or other adult food sources.

## How to Watch Them

People observe butterflies for a variety of reasons. Some may wish to explore their relationships with host plants. This will involve painstaking observations of females and searches for eggs and larvae on plants. Other people like to photograph butterflies. And many others are happy to just enjoy their presence and watch what they do. Collecting butterflies is not a satisfying pastime in Victoria, as most natural areas are in parks, where collecting is illegal. Besides, the Victoria area has been so well collected in the past that there is very little reason to collect any more. Collecting should always serve a purpose, usually to document the species present in a given area.

Whatever your purpose in pursuing butterflies, you will want to get close to them. There are several things to keep in mind if you are to avoid scaring off your quarry. Never allow your shadow to pass over a butterfly unless you are trying to make it fly. When approaching butterflies, they are less likely to scare if you keep your body low. Other tricks may be developed from observations of each species. For example, some butterflies are very territorial and will return to the same location after flying away. If you startle them, you need only step back and wait. Other species may have certain times of day that they are most approachable. Several species seek nectar intently in the late afternoon and are so focussed on their flowers that they ignore human observers. Experience with each species will teach you where, when and how close to approach each one.

## Keeping Records

A serious butterfly watcher should always record the butterflies he or she sees. The important information is where, when and which species. By keeping this information, a butterfly watcher can begin to build a list of where and when to go to see certain species. Also, the records can be checked against unusual records, like a species seen in a different location or time of

Clodius Apollo.

year than is expected. Most importantly, the records of individual naturalists can be used by the provincial and federal governments when they are trying to determine the status of a potentially rare butterfly species. For this reason, it is very important to keep detailed records of any at-risk butterfly species and report them to the British Columbia Conservation Data Centre (www.env.gov.bc.ca/cdc/). You will usually need photographs to confirm the record. Many of the butterflies now listed as at-risk were once considered common, and we know their past distribution only because past naturalists were recording common species. Record all butterflies in case this information becomes important in the future.

## Butterfly Habitats

Because each butterfly is associated with its own host plants, different habitat types support different species. The way to see many species, then, is to visit as many habitat types as possible throughout the year. The most common habitats in our area are residential areas, disturbed areas, hilltops with Garry Oak ecosystems and woodlands.

### Residential Areas
Residential gardens offer the easiest butterfly watching, both in terms of physical effort and the low number of species to be identified. Butterflies seen in residential areas are those species that can fly long distances to utilize gardens and ornamental trees.

Western Elfin.

Western Spring Azure.

The earliest butterfly to appear in residential areas is often the Cabbage White. This ubiquitous species was introduced to Quebec in the 1800s and arrived on the west coast about ten years after the railway. Its host plants include a huge variety of species in the cabbage family, including many garden vegetables. It has several generations per year in our area, and can be seen from March into October. As you are watching for it in the spring, keep an eye out for smaller butterflies such as the Western Elfin and Western Spring Azure. Both are regularly seen in residential areas, where their host plants may include several species of ornamental and native shrubs.

As the warm days of June set in, the black and yellow stripes of the Western Tiger Swallowtail become a regular sight in yards and even in the downtown core. This butterfly, the largest in our area, feeds largely on willows and related trees in the wild, but its larva can mature successfully on fruit trees and other ornamentals in residential areas.

Woodland Skipper.

Western Tiger Swallowtail.

If June belongs to the swallowtails, July is most certainly the domain of the Lorquin's Admiral. The brazen antics of this species add humour to any afternoon of butterfly watching. The males perch on branch tips and fly out to challenge all trespassers into their territory. They not only charge all other butterflies, but frequently fly at the faces of human intruders and will even charge toward the distant outline of a passing plane. At the same time that the admirals are flying, watch for the dull orange of the California Tortoiseshell. This migratory species has recently been recorded breeding on California Lilac in residential areas, and may be on its way to becoming a local resident.

If there is some long grass in your neighbourhood, the late summer will bring the Woodland Skipper. This small, fast butterfly reaches its peak in August, when butterfly numbers are beginning to decline. It is an avid visitor to flowers, especially purple ones.

## Disturbed Areas

Vacant lots, roadsides and rough areas around agricultural lands are often thick with weedy plants and the butterflies that can adapt to them. The Cabbage White is here, and so are two other species that are relative newcomers to the Victoria area. The Mylitta Crescent is a small checkered butterfly that breeds on thistles. This species is native to North America, and possibly even to British Columbia, but has expanded its range by following

Mylitta Crescent.

Purplish Copper.

introductions of non-native thistles. It reached the Victoria area in the 1950s and is now established over much of Vancouver Island. The Mylitta Crescent produces two broods per year, and can be seen from April to September. The European Skipper can be found in grassy disturbed areas, as well as natural meadows. This species was first recorded in Victoria in the 1990s by the Victoria Natural History Society. It is a European species that is proving extremely adaptable to different climates in British Columbia. It can now be found in the cool, wet north coast, the hot, dry interior, and the cold sub-boreal areas east of the Rocky Mountains. The European Skipper flies mainly in June. It decreases in abundance through July and is replaced by the abundant Woodland Skipper in August.

The Purplish Copper and Grey Hairstreak are unusual among the butterflies of disturbed habitats. Both may turn up anywhere at any time, but not in abundance and not always predictably. Their presence is never an expectation or a surprise. The Grey Hairstreak feeds on a great variety of weedy plants, especially legumes, while the Purplish Copper mainly uses docks (*Rumex* spp.), ubiquitous in disturbed areas.

The Silvery Blue, once common in Victoria, is now seen mainly along disturbed roadsides in the western communities. The Field Crescent is now found in just a few wet disturbed areas on the Saanich peninsula. It was once native to wet lowland meadows, which have been all but eliminated by urbanization and the introduction of Reed Canarygrass.

Field Crescent.

## Hilltops with Garry Oak Ecosystems

Rocky hilltops with Garry Oak, Arbutus and stunning spring flower displays are one of the most characteristic features of our city. They are also often the most productive areas for butterfly watching, especially in the spring. On the first warm days in March, a visit to the summit of Mount Douglas will be repaid with the sight of California Tortoiseshells just emerging from their winter hibernation. Some of these may be the progeny of successful breeding in residential areas the summer before. Some may be migrants that arrived in Victoria in the fall, just in time to find shelter for hibernation.

As the spring progresses further into March, the tortoiseshells at the top of the hill are joined by one of the most common companions of local hilltops, Anise Swallowtails. These butterflies require plants in the carrot family (*Apiaceae*) for larval hosts, and so are frequently to be found in Garry Oak meadows, where such plants abound. Further down the hill, they are joined by Pacific (Sara's) Orangetips and Moss's Elfins, two great lovers of rock outcrops, talus slopes and cliff faces. Moss's Elfin is sufficiently restricted in range to be of conservation concern in our area. In the Highlands and Sooke Hills, Shore Pine and Hairy Manzanita grow on many hilltops and support the Western Pine Elfin and Western Elfin, respectively. In these habitats, it is often possible to see all three of our elfin species flying together.

Another brown butterfly to watch for in the spring is the Propertius Duskywing, a large skipper. Like Moss's Elfin, the Propertius Duskywing is fairly common in Garry Oak woodlands, but is of conservation concern because it occurs in only a small area of British Columbia.

In summer the hilltops dry out so completely that there is little plant life to attract butterflies. Species that breed in the hills largely disappear until next spring. However, as the summer progresses, the hilltops become the best places in town to see many of our migratory species. Painted, West-coast and American ladies and Red Admirals disperse over great distances and employ an unusual strategy for finding mates. Males hold territories

Propertius Duskywing.

American Lady.

on hilltops, and unmated females have only to visit a hilltop to find a mate, then continue on their way. Open, isolated prominences like the summits of Mount Douglas and Mount Tolmie become the best places to see these species, even though there is no breeding habitat present. The butterflies on these hilltops are simply hopeful males. The Painted Lady is the most common. The Westcoast Lady and Red Admiral are seen more sporadically. Rarest among these species is the American Lady, recorded in late afternoons of late summer days every few years.

## Woodlands

The first and last butterflies of the year are often recorded at the edge of a woodland. The same species usually fills both positions – the orange-brown, ragged-edged Satyr Comma (Anglewing). Another common contender is the delightfully dark Mourning Cloak. Both species hibernate as adults and fly around sunny woodlands when the temperature permits. This can happen on any day of the year, and both of these species have been recorded in Victoria in at least ten of the twelve months. The Satyr Comma is only the most common representative of a group of similar species. Another the careful observer should watch for is the Green Comma, recognizable by the green spots on the underside of the wings.

As the spring weather starts to bring out other species, tiny brown Cedar Hairstreaks may sometimes be seen near forests that include their host plant, Western Redcedar. The use of conifers by butterflies is somewhat unusual, but this practise is shared by the Pine White. These butterflies float

Hilltop butterflies: Painted Lady (facing page) and Red Admiral (right).

Woodland species: Satyr Comma (below), Pine White (lower left) and Lorquin's Admiral (lower right).

like pieces of tissue paper in the canopy of Douglas-fir forests as the summer days begin to shorten. When they come down to seek nectar (often in the morning), the delicate patterning on the wings is revealed. They are not as white as they appear, but are traced with black lines along all the wing veins.

Between the seasons of the Cedar Hairstreak and Pine White, a host of other butterflies come and go in the sunny openings of our woodlands. Most noticeable for their size are the Western Tiger and Pale Swallowtails. In July, their perennial companion is Lorquin's Admiral, but they may also be joined by some of our nettle feeders, such as Red Admirals and Milbert's Tortoiseshells.

## Butterfly Conservation

Butterflies are ranked by the provincial and federal governments to determine which species are rare and at risk of extirpation. Southern Vancouver Island is one of the hot spots in British Columbia for butterflies at risk, with 16 species. Some of these species have not been seen in our area for

Pale Swallowtail (facing page) and Milbert's Tortoiseshell (right).

a long time, while others that are fairly common here have been found nowhere else in the country. An important step toward conserving our rare butterflies is to understand their life histories and needs, but there are other important steps that anyone can take.

## Habitat

By far the most important threat to butterflies is habitat destruction. In the Victoria area, any land that isn't already protected as in parks is in immediate danger of being converted into residential or commercial uses. The greatest threat to butterflies is the destruction of hilltops and Garry Oak ecosystems, where the majority of our rare butterflies are found. However, as described above, even agricultural or disturbed lands have some value to butterflies – all gone, though, if converted into malls and high-density neighbourhoods. If you want to contribute to butterfly conservation, the most important thing you can do is to support efforts to create new parks and protected areas.

Another major threat to our butterflies involves changes in plant communities that happen even in protected areas. Non-native plants are both diverse and abundant in our natural areas, and are sometimes the dominant species. Some of these plants have the potential to out-compete plants that are important in butterfly life cycles. Competition and resulting changes in the plant community can also alter butterfly habitats in the absence of non-native species. Before European settlement, the meadows and woodlands of the Victoria area experienced frequent, low-intensity fires. In the absence of these fires, diverse meadows and open woodlands have been replaced by denser forests and shrub thickets that have less value to butterflies.

## Gardening

In the years since George Taylor made his famous observations, Victoria has lost a great deal of its butterfly fauna. At the same time, Victoria has become known as the garden city. Clearly, conventional gardening has done little to

Lorquin's Admiral pupa.

slow the decline of our butterflies. In some cases, gardening has directly contributed to declines. But gardens have tremendous potential to provide benefit for butterflies if they are well planned.

The way to plan a butterfly garden is to learn which butterflies are likely to pass through your neighbourhood, learn their most likely host plants and emphasize these in your garden. Nectar sources should also be included, but are secondary in importance to the host plants. Avoid showy ornamental flowers, as the selective breeding that produces the size and colour is often at the expense of the nectaries (the glands that produce nectar). And do not plant a butterfly bush (*Buddleja* spp.), an invasive species. Any plant that has a negative effect on habitat cannot be a benefit to butterflies. Native species should always be favoured.

Remember that you are creating a home where butterflies will live year round. Even when you don't see them, eggs, larvae and pupae may be present. Therefore, avoid activities that are likely to remove or destroy these future butterflies. A clean, tidy garden is probably a death trap for butterflies.

## Btk (*Bacillus thuringiensis* var. *kurstaki*)

Spraying of the bacterial insecticide Btk to control the introduced Gypsy Moth has become a regular concern on Vancouver Island. People wonder how these spray programs may affect butterflies. Btk is lethal to moths and butterflies in general. There may be some natural variation in the effect on different species, but most species that are in their larval feeding stage while the pesticide is on foliage are expected to suffer high mortality. Species that are already rare will be affected the most, as they will be less able to recover quickly or recolonize from neighbouring areas. It's important that those implementing spray programs make an effort to determine whether rare species are present in the target area and modify their plans accordingly. Because the Gypsy Moth has the potential to cause great harm to our native ecosystems, this is a very difficult problem for conservationists.

# Checklist of Butterflies Recorded in the Victoria Area
## (to Sooke and Shawnigan Lake)

| Common Name | Species | Notes* |
|---|---|---|
| Silver-spotted Skipper | *Epargyreus clarus* | H |
| Northern Cloudywing | *Thorybes pylades* | H |
| Dreamy Duskywing | *Erynnis icelus* | H |
| Propertius Duskywing | *Erynnis propertius* | R |
| Persius Duskywing | *Erynnis persius* | H |
| Two-banded Checkered Skipper | *Pyrgus ruralis* | |
| Arctic Skipper | *Carterocephalus palaemon* | H |
| Western Branded Skipper | *Hesperia colorado* | R |
| European Skipper | *Thymelicus lineola* | I |
| Woodland Skipper | *Ochlodes sylvanoides* | |
| Dun Skipper | *Euphyes vestris* | H, R |
| Common Roadside Skipper | *Amblyscirtes vialis* | H |
| Clodius Apollo | *Parnassius clodius* | |
| Anise Swallowtail | *Papilio zelicaon* | |
| Western Tiger Swallowtail | *Papilio rutulus* | |
| Pale Swallowtail | *Papilio eurymedon* | |
| Pine White | *Neophasia menapia* | |
| Margined White | *Pieris marginalis* | H |
| Cabbage White | *Pieris rapae* | I |
| Island Marble | *Euchloe ausonides insulanus* | H, R |
| Pacific (Sara's) Orangetip | *Anthocaris sara* | |
| Orange Sulphur | *Colias eurytheme* | M |
| Western Sulphur | *Colias occidentalis* | R |
| Purplish Copper | *Lycaena helloides* | |
| Reakirt's Copper | *Lycaena mariposa* | H |
| Sylvan Hairstreak | *Satyrium sylvinum* | H |
| Cedar Hairstreak | *Mitoura rosneri* | |
| Johnson's Hairstreak | *Loranthomitoura johnsoni* | H, R |
| Western Elfin | *Incisalia iroides* | |
| Moss's Elfin | *Incisalia mossii* | R |
| Western Pine Elfin | *Incisalia eryphon* | R |
| Grey Hairstreak | *Strymon melinus* | |
| Western Tailed Blue | *Everes amyntula* | H |
| Western Spring Azure | *Celastrina echo* | |
| Silvery Blue | *Glaucopsyche lygdamus* | |
| Anna's Blue | *Lycaeides anna* | H |

* H= Historic records only.
  R= Listed as a species at risk provincially or federally.
  M= Migratory species (not resident).
  I=Introduced species.

| Common Name | Species | Notes* |
|---|---|---|
| Island Blue | *Plebejus insulanus saepiolus* | H, R |
| Boisduval's Blue | *Icaricia icarioides* | H, R |
| Satyr Comma (Anglewing) | *Polygonia satyrus* | |
| Green Comma | *Polygonia faunus* | |
| Zephyr Anglewing | *Polygonia zephyrus* | H |
| Oreas Anglewing | *Polygonia oreas* | H |
| Milbert's Tortoiseshell | *Aglais milberti* | |
| Mourning Cloak | *Nymphalis antiopa* | |
| California Tortoiseshell | *Nymphalis californica* | M |
| American Lady | *Vanessa virginiensis* | M |
| Painted Lady | *Vanessa cardui* | M |
| Westcoast Lady | *Vanessa annabella* | M |
| Red Admiral | *Vanessa atalanta* | M |
| Zerene Fritillary | *Speyeria zerene* | H, R |
| Hydaspe Fritillary | *Speyeria hydaspe* | |
| Western Meadow Fritillary | *Clossiana epithore* | H |
| Field Crescent | *Phyciodes pratensis* | |
| Mylitta Crescent | *Phyciodes mylitta* | |
| Chalcedon Checkerspot | *Euphydryas chalcedona* | H |
| Taylor's Checkerspot | *Euphydryas editha* | H, R |
| Lorquin's Admiral | *Limenitis lorquini* | |
| Common Ringlet | *Coenonympha californica* | R |
| Common Woodnymph | *Cercyonis pegala* | R |
| Great Arctic | *Oeneis nevadensis* | R |
| Monarch | *Danaus plexippus* | M, R |

\* H= Historic records only.
 R= Listed as a species at risk provincially or federally.
 M= Migratory species (not resident).
 I=Introduced species.

Great Arctic.

# Dragonflies

## Robert Cannings

## Dragonfly Biology

Dragonflies have fascinated people all over the world and down through the ages with their bright colours and dashing flight. A patient observer can easily watch dragonflies going about their lives. They are large insects, colourful and easy to find, if you know where to look. As adults, they are active by day and, with a little practice, many of them can be identified in the field. Of the 87 species known to live in British Columbia, 49 are recorded in the Victoria region.

Since the 1990s, especially, more and more people who love the outdoors have become interested in dragonflies. This has sparked an increase in popular books on dragonflies and a proliferation of Internet sites dealing with these insects. Not only is the popularity of watching dragonflies on the rise, biologists are studying them more and more, often because they are excellent indicators of ecosystem health. Dragonflies are ecologically important for many reasons. They are upper-level predators in aquatic and semi-aquatic habitats, often dominating the large invertebrates, especially in places where there are no fish. They usually inhabit the edges of water bodies, living as larvae in shallow water and as adults mostly in the zone between dry land and open water. Many species live only in particular habitats and their presence can be used to characterize healthy wetlands of all sorts. Unlike most invertebrates, adult dragonflies and damselflies can be identified in the field, many even by beginners, and so they are well-suited to long-term monitoring programs. Finally, because these large, colourful diurnal creatures have interesting behaviours and are easy to watch, and because the aquatic larvae can readily be kept in captivity for observation, they are excellent subjects for nature interpretation programs and public education about aquatic ecosystems in general.

The insect order Odonata (Greek for "toothed jaws") contains both the groups of insects known in English as the dragonflies and damselflies, but

Canada Darner eating a meadowhawk.

here I use the name "dragonflies" to refer to the whole order. The term "odonates" is also becoming a popular term for these insects, mainly because if "dragonfly" is restricted to the Anisoptera (see below), there is no English word for the Odonata as a whole.

The Odonata is a small order of insects of about 5,500 named species and 33 families worldwide. For comparison, there are roughly the same number of mammal species in the world and almost twice as many birds. In North America, the Odonata includes two suborders – the Zygoptera (damselflies), and the Anisoptera (true dragonflies). Damselflies are slimmer, often smaller, and usually fly more slowly than dragonflies. At rest their equal-sized wings are usually held together above the body (the spreadwing family is an exception). Zygoptera means "joined wings". True dragonflies are robust, often fast-flying, with the hindwings broader than the forewings. Anisoptera means "unequal wings". When perched they hold their wings out away from the body.

Dragonflies are ancient insects; the earliest of their direct ancestors flew in the Carboniferous Period, about 300 to 350 million years ago. They have retained many primitive characteristics but also possess specialized features that reflect a successful aerial and predatory life. Dragonflies share with mayflies the ancient inability to fold their wings flat over the body. They differ from all other insects in their combination of biting mouthparts, their two equal (or almost equal) pairs of long, membranous, net-veined wings; their large, bulging eyes and short, thread-like antennae, and their long, slender abdomen that, in the male, bears secondary genitalia at the base.

Most dragonfly species are tropical but many live in temperate zones and a few are adapted to the cold temperatures of higher latitudes. All dragonflies have aquatic larvae and live around most types of freshwater. They are large and abundant insects and, because of this, they are a predominant component of freshwater communities, at least those in standing water, in the Victoria region. Certain kinds prefer small ponds and warm, marshy lakeshores; others live mostly in colder lakes; some are found only along streams or in peatlands. Warm ponds and marshes rich in aquatic vegetation support the most species.

The aquatic larva grows and moults many times (usually 10 to 14) depending on the species and the environmental conditions. For many species in British Columbia, the life cycle takes about a year. Many species

Larva of a Four-spotted Skimmer (above) and an emerging Variable Darner.

overwinter as larvae and emerge the following spring or summer, but some spreadwings and meadowhawks that live in temporary ponds overwinter as eggs, hatch in the spring, grow rapidly and emerge as adults in the summer. Still other species spend more than one year in the larval stage. For some dragonflies (especially certain darners and emeralds), the larval life may last six years or longer. Development time depends on the species and also on altitude, latitude, and amount of daylight.

The aquatic larvae are voracious predators. Armed with an enormous hinged labium, a sort of lower lip used as an extendible grasping organ for capturing prey, they eat small aquatic insects, crustaceans and even fish. Larvae can be placed in three categories according to their body structure and feeding behaviour: *claspers* (damselflies and darners) climb the stems and leaves of submerged vegetation in search of prey; *sprawlers* (cruisers, emeralds, and skimmers) lie in ambush on the bottom mud and debris; and *burrowers* (clubtails and spiketails) cover themselves with sand and mud and await their prey.

Unlike butterflies and many other insects, dragonflies have no pupal stage. A fully grown larva metamorphoses into an adult inside its last larval skin, then crawls out of the water, up a plant stalk or other support. Clubtails and pond damsels can emerge horizontally on rocks, floating logs and plants, or right on the sand or mud. The top of the larval thorax splits open and the adult dragonfly squeezes out of the skin. It pumps blood into its wings and abdomen, which expand slowly, and gradually the body hardens.

Striped Meadowhawks mating.

The adult dragonfly will not grow larger even though it eats a lot. An hour or two after it emerges, the dragonfly can fly, weakly at first, on fragile, glistening wings. It leaves the empty larval skin (the exuvia) clinging to the support. The newly emerged adult, called a teneral, is vulnerable to predators and bad weather. Immature adults are pale in colour, but gradually become darker and often brighter as they mature. Some species produce a waxy, white or pale blue powder, called pruinescence, over parts of the body and wings; this is especially obvious in some male skimmers and spread-wings and some female forktails.

After emergence, most adults leave the shoreline to hunt and eat for a few days or even weeks as they mature. They are powerful predators that hunt by sight. They usually capture prey while flying, grabbing it with long, spiny legs and then chewing it with powerful jaws. Adult dragonflies eat mainly flying insects, but some species will pluck insects, spiders and even small frogs off vegetation or the ground.

The flying ability of dragonflies amazes most people. Although the wing structure and arrangement of the flight muscles are primitive, the flight performance and efficiency are remarkable. Unlike most insects, dragonflies usually beat their forewings and hindwings separately – when the forewings are up, the hindwings are down. Each wing also has much independent control, accounting for the surprising manoeuvrability of many species, which can fly upwards, sideways, backwards, and forwards. A large darner can fly up to 60 km per hour. Darners, emeralds, spiketails, river cruisers and some skimmers are called *flyers* because they spend most of their active life flying – they even generate additional body heat from their wing muscles. Damselflies, clubtails, and most skimmers are often called *perchers*, because they spend more time perching than flying. Perchers gain much of their body heat from basking in the sun and make only short flights to mate or catch food.

For millennia, dragonflies have instilled superstitious fear in humans, even though they do not sting or bite people. Maybe their boldness takes us aback, or their speed startles us. To the uninitiated, their strange appearance up close can make them seem fearsome. The English name "dragonfly" echoes the feelings these insects sometimes arouse – they are the fanciful "devil's darning needles" that sting people or sew up their lips; they are "snake doctors" with the power to bring dead snakes back to life. These legends and folktales are groundless – dragonflies are harmless to humans.

When they are sexually mature, dragonflies return to the water to breed. Most of the dragonflies you

A mating pair of Northern Spreadwings laying eggs.

see near water are males aggressively searching for mates. In many species (damselflies, petaltails, clubtails, emeralds and many skimmers), mature males defend a territory against other males of the species, patrolling the habitat or sallying out from perches. This territorial behaviour limits aggression by spacing males along the shore and helps prevent undue disturbance of egg-laying females.

Females coming to the water to breed quickly attract mates. With the appendages at the tip of the abdomen, a male grasps a female by the front of the thorax (damselflies) or by the top of the head (true dragonflies). This head to tail arrangement is called the tandem position. Before joining with a female or even while in the tandem position, the male transfers sperm from the tip of his abdomen to his penis, which is under the second abdominal segment. The female then loops the end of her abdomen up to the base of the male's abdomen so that the sperm can be transferred. Dragonflies are the only insects that mate in this circular formation, called the wheel position, which they maintain for a few seconds or several hours, depending on the species.

The female lays her fertilized eggs by the hundreds. All damselflies, darners and petaltails have a knifelike egg-laying structure with pointed blades (the ovipositor) at the tip of the abdomen; they lay their eggs in plant tissue, although some darners and petaltails insert eggs into mud. Spiketails shovel their eggs into a streambed. Other species simply drop eggs into the

Female Paddle-tailed Darner laying eggs.

water, tap the eggs into mud and moss, or dip the tip of the abdomen into the water and wash the eggs off.

Competition for mates is usually fierce, and male aggression can prevent females from laying their eggs. Females that lay their eggs alone, especially mosaic darners and many emeralds, often do so stealthily, flying low among the plants along the shore, wings rustling in the stems as they settle to deposit the eggs. Some damselflies actually crawl below the water's surface to escape the attention of males, often remaining submerged for more than an hour. They take a film of air down with them, trapped in the hairs on their body, so they can breathe while they lay their eggs. In many damselflies, the meadowhawks, and the Common Green Darner, the male normally stays in tandem, retaining his hold on the female while she lays her eggs. In some other species, the male hovers protectively nearby, guarding the egg-laying female from any other males who may attempt to mate with her. This helps ensure that the male's sperm will fertilize the eggs being laid and allows the female to lay her eggs undisturbed.

# Dragonfly Habitats and Their Typical Species

Dragonflies live in many freshwater habitats and, with practice, you can predict many of the species you will see when visiting different types of water bodies. Below are the general types of habitats where dragonflies live in the Victoria region. The species mentioned for each habitat typically breed and develop in these places, but some may have special characteristics that discourage certain species. Places with a mixture of habitat types usually have the greatest diversity of species. And of course, abundant species and those with prominent behaviours are more easily seen than less common species or those that skulk in the vegetation. This is a general outline only and is not foolproof. What you see also will depend on when you visit – many species can be found only at certain times of the season. Not all the species known in the region are mentioned in these accounts. See the species checklist (pages 76-77) for a complete list.

## Freshwater Marshes

These still-water habitats occur mostly in warm lowland areas and are characterized by permanent or seasonal flooding of nutrient-rich waters. Some are artificial, but others have been destroyed because they occur in urbanized areas where they are not wanted. Marshes – including the marshy margins of lakes and ponds – are rich in plant and animal life and are the dragonfly habitats that most dragonfly observers will visit. These environments are dominated by cattails, rushes, sedges and grasses, and commonly support diverse populations of other aquatic plants such as pondweeds, water-lilies, water plantains, cinquefoils and bur-reeds. Such marshes also usually support the most diverse dragonfly assemblages.

Well-known localities include Swan Lake, Beaver Lake and the adjacent Retriever Ponds, King's Pond, Quick's Bottom, Viaduct Flats, Spencer Pond (Langford) and park ponds such as those at the gardens at Royal Roads University and in Beacon Hill Park. Dozens of other ponds in farms, golf courses and gardens belong to this habitat type.

Viaduct Flats.

Among the damselflies in these habitats, the three genera to look for are the spreadwings, American bluets and forktails; red damsels can also be found in the region. Spreadwings are large damselflies, brown, black, metallic-green or bronze above. As their name suggests, they hold the wings half-spread when resting and, as they age, parts of the body, including the tip of the abdomen in males, often become powdery white. Females lay eggs in tandem with males, usually in plants above the surface of the water. Northern, Emerald, and Spotted spreadwings are common but Lyre-tipped and Sweetflag spreadwings are harder to find. At any one place, adults of the different species usually begin flying in sequence – Emerald, late May; Lyre-tipped, early June; Northern, mid June; Spotted, early July.

Unlike spreadwings, species in the pond damsel family normally perch with wings closed above the abdomen. Most are blue marked with black, but the main colour may be green, yellow, orange, red or purple. There are often two female colour forms, one of which is similar to the male (usually blue). Females lay eggs in the tissues of water plants, sometimes completely submerging themselves for considerable periods while depositing eggs. Northern and Boreal bluets are common around Victoria although the former is usually seen more frequently, especially in warmer waters. Both fly well into October, after first appearing early in the year – Boreal Bluets in April and Northerns in early May. The two are hard to distinguish without examining them closely and females can be especially tricky.

Male forktails are mostly black, blue and green. The abdomen is black on top and has a blue tip; the last segment bears a distinct forked projection on top, which gives the group its English name. Females may be the same colour as males or may have a tan, pink or orange thorax when immature; they may darken with extensive pruinescence as they age.

The Pacific Forktail is probably the most common and widespread odonate in the Victoria area. It lives in every garden pond, no matter how small, and flies around marshy places everywhere. The male has two distinctive pairs of small pale blue spots on top of the thorax. It has one of the longest flight seasons of any dragonfly in British Columbia (early April to late October) and is usually the first to appear in spring. Western Forktails are also common in marshy places; males have green stripes on top of the thorax. The stocky females are completely covered by a grey-white pruinescence when mature and lay eggs alone, their grey bodies and green eyes making identification easy. The larger Swift Forktail is found only on the south coast in BC. Most often seen in May and June around Victoria, it is less common than the Pacific and Western forktails. Unlike these other forktails, however, it is well adapted to many peatland habitats.

The Western Red Damsel is the only damselfly in the region (and in BC) whose adults are red in both sexes. The adults have stubby abdomens and short legs. The species prefers shallow marshy places with plenty of grasses and sedges. It is uncommon around Victoria, but good spots to find it are Quick's Bottom, Viaduct Flats and Rithet's Bog.

Male Blue-eyed Darner.                    Male Eight-spotted Skimmer.

The most striking species of true dragonflies common around lowland ponds and marshes are Blue-eyed and California darners, the Eight-spotted Skimmer, the Cardinal Meadowhawk and the Blue Dasher.

Darners are large, swift-flying dragonflies usually marked with blue, green or yellow. Adults hunt tirelessly for insects over ponds, lakes and streams, and wander widely in search of prey. Most species rest in a vertical position, but a few sit flat on the ground. Females have a prominent ovipositor and lay eggs in water plants or floating wood above or below the water line.

The Blue-eyed Darner male has sky-blue eyes and face and is one of Victoria's most abundant dragonflies in midsummer. Its close relative, the California Darner, is smaller and appears much earlier in the same habitats – ponds, lakes and marshes at low and medium elevations. For a darner, the species is remarkable for its springtime flight season. It appears in April, with the earliest dragonflies; by early August it is uncommon, just when many other darners are reaching their peak abundance. The largest of our local dragonflies, the Common Green Darner, is less often seen than its name suggests but, especially in late summer, it flies powerfully back and forth over the water in these habitats.

The skimmers are the largest dragonfly family in the Victoria region. They come in many sizes and colours, many with bold wing markings or coloured veins. Their eyes meet broadly on top of the head. Most common around ponds, marshy lakeshores and sluggish streams, the adults dart about and most species spend a lot of time perched horizontally in the sun.

Most king skimmers have banded or spotted wings, and males in some species sport abdomens covered with white or bluish pruinescence. During egg laying, a female taps the water with the end of her abdomen; she flies alone or is guarded by her mate hovering nearby. The Eight-spotted Skimmer has two large dark patches on each wing; mature males and some females have white patches between the dark ones and near the wing tips, which are clear. The Four-spotted Skimmer is less showy – each wing bears a small dark spot at the midpoint of the front edge, and the hindwings have a dark triangular patch at the base. A golden stripe on the front edge of

Cardinal Meadowhawk.

each wing can be prominent or vague. One of the earliest dragonflies in the spring, this species is common around the whole northern hemisphere.

The Common Whitetail shows striking differences between the sexes. The male has a broad dark-brown band across each wing; when mature, its broad abdomen is covered with bright white pruinescence. The female has brown wingtips, and patches at the base and in the middle of each wing. This attractive species typically perches on the ground or on low twigs, but it is less common around Victoria than Eight-spotted and Four-spotted skimmers.

The Blue Dasher is a small to medium-sized skimmer; the mature male is easily recognized by its white face, green eyes and abdomen thickly coated with pale blue pruinescence. Males hover frequently and defend territories aggressively; they perch, with wings cocked downward, on stems and twigs. Young Western Pondhawks are grass-green with clear wings; males turn blue with pruinescence as they age, but females remain green. Pondhawks usually perch flat on the ground or on floating vegetation.

The Dot-tailed Whiteface features a distinctive yellow spot – actually, a pair of dots – on its abdomen. On mature males, this spot stands out against the dark body, as does the white face. Immature males, many mature females and very few mature males have yellow on other segments of the abdomen. Unlike other whitefaces, the Dot-tailed is most at home in warm lowland waters. It is common in ponds and the marshy corners of lakes; it likes organically rich places such as farmyard ponds.

Meadowhawks are small to medium-sized dragonflies that are mostly yellow when young and mostly red when mature. Females are usually yellow or tan, but can be red like males. Usually you can observe adults easily at close range, because most species are not powerful fliers and perch often. They are frequently abundant around ponds and lakes and adjacent meadows, especially in the late summer and fall. Many species often perch on the ground. Eight meadowhawk species live in the Victoria region. The Cardinal Meadowhawk is the most noticeable – it is the largest species, brilliant scarlet with brown marks at the base of the wings, and common around ponds. It begins flying in May, well before most other meadowhawk species are visible. The Striped Meadowhawk is the most abundant late summer and fall species. It has a yellow face, a pair of yellow-white stripes on the sides of the thorax, and usually a smaller pair on top, and saw-toothed black stripes on the sides of the abdomen.

The Black Saddlebags is spectacular gliding overhead; the black bases of its broad hind wings are a clear field mark. This wandering species appeared in British Columbia for the first time in 1995 and has been seen every year since, especially in August. In 2006 a mating pair was photographed and it probably now breeds successfully in warm ponds in the area. Viaduct Flats is a particularly good place to see it.

## Small Lakes and Ponds in Forests or on Hills

Forest lakes and ponds often have a mixture of habitats around their margins, and support dragonfly species that are also common in the warm, marshy habitats described above. But other small lakes and ponds, away from open areas or at higher elevations around Victoria, have colder waters that suit a different group of species. These water bodies support floating plants, such as water lilies, but few have much emergent vegetation around their shores. They may be deep and rock-edged or they may have peaty edges. Sedges or cattails may grow in some marginal areas. A number of species are typical in these small lakes and ponds: Northern Spreadwing;

Small lake north of Jordan River.

Lake Darner.                              Mating pair of American Emeralds.

Boreal Bluet; Blue-eyed, Canada, Lake, Paddle-tailed and Shadow darners; Spiny Baskettail; American and Ringed emeralds; Crimson-ringed, Hudsonian and Belted whitefaces; Chalk-fronted Corporal; Four-spotted Skimmer; and Autumn and White-faced meadowhawks.

The Paddle-tailed Darner is abundant around Victoria's lakes from late June to early November. Its face is greenish yellow with a black line and the thorax stripes are almost straight. Males of the Paddle-tailed Darner and the closely related Shadow Darner have flat appendages at the end of the abdomen; the Shadow Darner is greener and has a pale brown face line. It is one of the last species to disappear in the fall, sometimes lasting until the second week of November. Around Victoria and on the coast in general, males of the Variable Darner have distinctly broken thorax stripes; interior populations normally have complete stripes. This variation is what gives the species its English name. Our largest darner, the Lake Darner, is one of the most often encountered dragonflies in the northern forests of North America. It prefers lakeshores with little emergent vegetation but also occurs in deep fens and bogs, and around lakes and ponds surrounded by sedges. It may fly early in the morning and in the evening when the temperature is cool and the light is low. It likes perching on tree trunks.

Emeralds are medium-sized dragonflies most often seen around lakes, boggy streams and peatlands in the mountains. The eyes, often brilliant green, meet broadly on top of the head. Adults seldom perch during feeding and males frequently hover when patrolling for mates; when resting,

Male Chalk-fronted
Corporal.

they hang vertically or obliquely from vegetation. The American Emerald's thorax is metallic green-bronze and has no pale marks on the sides and the abdomen is mostly black. The most commonly seen emerald around Victoria, this species flies early in the season, especially in June and early July. Males patrol energetically and aggressively around forest lakes, chasing off males of their own and other species. The Mountain Emerald may also be found in these habitats, especially where sedges grow.

Rather than metallic green and black like other emeralds, baskettails have a brown thorax and a dark abdomen with yellow marks on the sides. The hindwings are marked with brown at the base. Females fly with the end of the abdomen curled upwards, the forked tip holding a ball of eggs as in a basket, which gives the group its English name. To lay the eggs, a female dips the egg mass into the water and it uncoils in long, gelatinous strands that float near the surface. Many females may contribute to communal egg masses. The Spiny Baskettail flies early in the season around Victoria – it's usually seen in May and June hunting overhead, often in groups.

Mature Chalk-fronted Corporals have distinctive pale pruinescence on the front of the thorax and the base of abdomen. The wings are clear except for small, dark marks at the bases; those on the hindwings are triangular. This dragonfly likes slightly acidic waters and flies around peaty forest ponds and swampy lake bays, especially in early summer. In some years it can swarm. Unlike king skimmers, this species often rests on rocks, logs, floating water-lily leaves or bare ground.

White-faces are small, black, white-faced dragonflies marked with red or yellow and the hindwings have a distinctive small, triangular dark patch at the base. They perch on the ground, logs, lily pads or low vegetation. Males usually hover nearby while females lay eggs. Hudsonian, Crimson-ringed and Belted whitefaces live around forest and mountain lakes and marshes in the Victoria region, although the Belted Whiteface is uncommon.

The Autumn Meadowhawk is distinctive for its lack of body markings. Immatures are yellow-brown with unmarked yellow legs; mature males and some females become mostly red with red-brown legs. Rather uncommon around Victoria, this meadowhawk lives mostly in forest ponds and small lakes at low to mid elevations. Matheson and Blinkhorn lakes in Metchosin are good places to see it. It flies later than any other dragonfly in the province, in some years until mid November.

## Sedge Marshes

Sedges are common grass-like plants that grow up to 150 cm tall in dense stands around lakes and ponds or in large areas of shallow water. Although sedges occur almost everywhere near water, this account deals with marshes at medium and high elevations in the region. Typical dragonfly species in these habitats are: Common, Emerald, Spotted and Sweetflag spreadwings; Boreal and Northern bluets; Paddle-tailed, Sedge and Variable darners; Mountain Emerald; Four-spotted Skimmer; Hudsonian Whiteface; and White-faced Meadowhawk.

The Sweetflag Spreadwing, especially the male, is extremely similar to the Common Spreadwing. Identification is best done with the female, whose large, distinctive ovipositor extends beyond the end of the abdomen. In the Victoria region it has been found only in the Spectacle Lake area so far.

The Sedge Darner is scarce in the Victoria area. It is probably restricted to higher elevations in the hills, but likely is more widespread than the few records indicate. The Mountain Emerald is widespread in the region, especially in the hills. The sides of the thorax are shiny metallic green with two oval yellow spots, the larger in front. Viewed from above, the tip of the male's abdomen looks like a pincer. This species prefers marshes, lakes and ponds where the sedges are tall and dense; males patrol and hover over these sedge beds. Another sedge dweller, also found in other habitats, is the White-faced Meadowhawk. The male is red with a white face, an unmarked thorax and black saw-toothed side stripes on the abdomen.

## Temporary Ponds

The best examples of species adapted to temporary ponds that dry up in summer are: Emerald, Lyre-tipped and Spotted spreadwings, and Red-veined, Saffron-winged, Striped and Variegated meadowhawks. Some of these species overwinter as eggs in the dry pond basin. The larvae appear in the spring and grow rapidly; adult emergence is often concentrated in a short time, before the waters disappear.

The Red-veined Meadowhawk is seen regularly in the Victoria area. It lives in a range of habitats, including Spencer Pond in Langford and the narrow marshy depressions behind the beach at Witty's Lagoon. Females drop eggs into the water or on the beds of dry pools. Immatures are grey-brown but males and some females become red, darkening to wine red with age. The sides of the thorax have two white stripes that shrink to spots in mature males. The wing veins are yellow, turning red with age; old specimens have brown-tinted wing membranes. Spencer Pond has the distinction of being the place where, in 1979, the larva was first discovered.

Belted Whitefaces mating (top), male
Four-spotted Skimmer (left), male Red-
veined Meadowhawk (above) and
Spencer Pond (below).

Male Mountain Emerald.

Peatland on San Juan Ridge.

# Peatlands

Peatlands are aquatic or semi-aquatic habitats where plant decomposition is so slow that peat accumulates. Bogs are acidic, low-nutrient peatlands whose water comes only from rain and snow; they are dominated by sphagnum mosses. Fens are peatlands affected by flowing ground water and, thus, richer in minerals and less acidic than bogs; they are dominated by sedges, grasses and non-sphagnum mosses. Northern and Sweetflag spreadwings, Boreal Bluets, Black-tipped and Zigzag darners, Mountain and Ringed emeralds, Black Meadowhawks, and Hudsonian Whitefaces are typical peatland dragonflies.

The Zigzag Darner is small, with narrow, zigzagged thorax stripes; the male's abdomen has large blue spots. It inhabits specific peatlands, where it can be abundant: bogs or fens where the surface is mossy and sparsely vegetated with short, evenly spaced sedges, and where open water, if present, is reduced to small, shallow mud- or moss-bottomed ponds and puddles. Adults perch on the ground, rocks and logs, or vertically on the low parts of tree trunks. The Black-tipped Darner is another species with only one or two records in the region, but it probably breeds in suitable fens across the northern half of the area. This large and slender dragonfly has straight, broad green-to-blue thorax stripes. The tip of its abdomen is all black, as the English name indicates. The female is coloured like the male. Females patrol their territories like males and often lay eggs in vegetation above the waterline. Presumably, this behaviour reduces the amount of attention that males give them, allowing more time for uninterrupted egg-laying.

In the Victoria region the striped emeralds are best seen around peat-margined lakes, boggy streams and mossy peatlands. The medium-sized adults usually have metallic blackish-green or brassy bodies. Three species have been seen in the area and a fourth is expected. The Ringed Emerald is a common coastal species that lives in forest lakes, subalpine ponds with firm edges, and coastal bogs. The peatlands of San Juan Ridge are good places to see it. The Mountain Emerald lives in sedge marshes and sedgy peatlands. The Ocellated Emerald is a rare inhabitant of forest and peatland streams in

Male Ringed Emerald.

the hills north of Victoria. The Brush-tipped Emerald should be there, too, but has not yet been recorded.

The Black Meadowhawk is the only meadowhawk in our region with no red on it. Mature males are almost all black; females also turn mostly black, but usually not as much as males. Immatures have yellow lines and spots on the sides of the thorax and the abdomen is black with pairs of yellow spots on the top. In the Victoria region this species is restricted to peatland pools such as those on the San Juan Ridge.

## Large Lakes

Although there are no large lakes in the Victoria region, there are some in adjacent areas such as Shawnigan and Sooke, and a few reservoirs that have portions of their shorelines wave-washed with little aquatic vegetation. These habitats support only a few dragonfly species, such as the Tule Bluet, Lake Darner and Shadow Darner. In shallow waters in sheltered bays, where marsh vegetation may occur, the species are usually the same as those found in small lakes or ponds.

Goldstream River.

Male Tule Bluet.

## Streams

Few dragonfly species develop in the cold mountain streams of British Columbia. Those that do are restricted to streams flowing from lakes or peatlands where the surface water has been warmed by the sun. The Victoria region has its share of such creeks and rivers, but stream-dwelling species are few. The most obvious is the Pacific Spiketail, a large black-and-yellow dragonfly. Adult males patrol up and down these streams with a steady flight, searching for mates. Females have a spade-like ovipositor and, hovering vertically, shove eggs into the sand and silt of the streambed. The Goldstream River is a good place to see spiketails locally, although they also breed in much smaller forest streams.

The Shadow Darner is common around forest lakes and streams, especially in the fall. The Ocellated Emerald has only been seen at the source of the Goldstream River, but must occur widely in the north part of the region. Though it has not been recorded here yet, the Sinuous Snaketail might be found soon by a keen observer. This clubtail is common along the rocky banks of the Nanaimo River and has been collected at Sahtlam on the Cowichan. There are many suitable sites for it on the Koksilah River and southward, though it's not likely to be found in the region's western drainages where the climate is probably too cool and wet.

Male Pacific Spiketail.

# Dragonfly Conservation

The most critical problem for dragonflies today is the destruction or alteration of their freshwater habitats. In the Victoria region the most damaging human activity is the draining and filling of marshes and ponds. So far, this has probably not eliminated any species from the region, but in some places it has reduced the populations of many species, including: Northern and Boreal bluets; Pacific and Western forktails; Blue-eyed, California and Variable darners; Mountain Emerald; Western Pondhawk; Eight-spotted Skimmer; Blue Dasher; Dot-tailed White-face; and Cardinal, Red-veined, Striped and Autumn meadowhawks. On the positive side, the creation of artificial ponds and small lakes has increased the numbers of many of these species in urban and suburban environments that were once heavily forested.

The destruction of natural lakeshores during the construction of houses, swimming beaches and roads also reduces dragonfly habitats. Logging and associated road building can result in streams with less stable flows, warmer water temperatures and higher silt loads, all of which negatively affect dragonfly larvae. Logging can also damage dragonfly communities in peatlands, marshes and lakes, especially at higher elevations. Extensive logging has affected dozens of streams in the region and probably reduced the populations of dragonflies such as the Shadow Darner, Sinuous Snaketail, Pacific Spiketail and Ocellated Emerald.

The dams created for hydroelectric power, flood control and water storage that have destroyed many wetlands throughout British Columbia are not such a destructive force in the Victoria region, though a number of lakes here have been dammed, Sooke Lake being the largest. Water reservoirs, by their nature, have fluctuating waterlines and are poor dragonfly habitat. Their construction may also damage stable peatlands, ponds, shallow lakes and slow streams, so reducing dragonfly habitat. In our area, such habitat loss has probably eliminated populations of peatland-dwelling species, such as Zigzag and Black-tipped darners, and several emeralds. Assuming shorelines lack extensive marshy or peatland edges, these uncommon species are replaced with a few common widespread species, such as Lake and Shadow darners.

Fish are major predators of dragonfly larvae, and the releasing of sport fish into some of the region's lakes (some originally fish-free) likely had a significant effect on both the abundance of dragonflies and the composition of the communities in these lakes. The poisoning of lakes to prepare them for sport-fish introductions has also likely had a significant impact on dragonfly populations. And the aquatic communities of many systems that historically contained fish have been altered by the purposeful or accidental introduction of non-native fish species. Some of these species not only eat many dragonfly larvae, but also alter the habitat structure.

Global climate change will affect the distribution of dragonfly habitats in our region. Especially in summer, there will be less water available in most areas as temperatures and evaporation increase. A significant component of the diversity of local dragonflies lives in marshes and small lakes in the lowlands. Presumably, many of these habitats will disappear in any drying trend. Groundwater will play a more important role than it does today, and more ponds will perhaps become more alkaline. The additional nutrients will change water chemistry. Peatlands will become more marshy and the special fauna of bogs and fens at higher elevations in the northern part of the region will likely decline.

Whether dragonfly populations will be able to shift northward or to higher altitudes if suitable water bodies remain there is unknown, but the relatively strong powers of dispersal of many species, at least, should be a major factor in their survival. A few southern species continue to move north. The Widow Skimmer (*Libellula luctuosa*) may arrive in the region before long; it has been expanding its range north from California and has been spotted north of the Columbia River. Other species have already appeared – Black Saddlebags and Spot-winged Glider, both well known for their wide-ranging flights, have been recorded in the region. Black Saddlebags has appeared annually since 1995 and observations of a mating pair suggest that it may successfully breed locally.

What can we do? We must learn more about our dragonflies so that we can protect them and their habitats. But also we must act quickly to protect the natural communities where dragonflies live. Small ponds, marshes, springs and streams on southern Vancouver Island sustain some uncommon species, and these habitats are among the first to disappear when we expand housing, industrial and agricultural developments. Even in remote areas, sensitive aquatic ecosystems can be drastically affected by industrial activity. Suitable dragonfly habitats are disappearing faster than new ones are being formed, so there is increasing cause for concern.

We can get involved with local naturalist organizations to learn more about the natural world in our neighbourhoods. We can encourage all levels of government to protect aquatic ecosystems on public land. We can get involved in public processes to develop land-use plans and regulations that preserve, rather than destroy, natural diversity. And we can maintain and create natural habitats on our own property. Build a pond in your garden or on your farm (ponds without fish are best) and see what arrives. Learn about the dragonflies and other creatures that settle there and encourage others to do the same.

# Watching Dragonflies

Look carefully at the size, shape and colour of the dragonflies. Concentrate on a particular individual. How does it fly? How does it perch? How does it hold its wings? Are the eyes widely separated? What colours and patterns do you see? Some species are very similar to others, so small details are important. Binoculars are useful for field identification; pick a pair with a magnification around 8× that focuses closer than 2.5 metres (8 ft). While you are learning the species, the best way to identify a dragonfly is to catch it in an insect net and identify it in the hand. Gently hold the wings together between finger and thumb, with the wings over its back; this will not harm the insect. But *do not hold* a teneral (recently emerged) dragonfly – you will damage its wings. You may have to use a hand lens to see some features well. Look at it carefully and release it after you have made your identification. A few books are designed for use in British Columbia (see the suggested readings list at the back of this book), or you can photograph your specimen and compare it to the hundreds that you can find on the Internet. There

The correct way to hold a live dragonfly.

are many good websites to help in identification and other aspects of dragonfly study.

We still have a lot to learn about dragonflies, like the geographical distribution of many species. We need more thorough descriptions of the behaviour of many species in our region, as well as carefully documented details about adult and larval habitat preferences and long-term observations of species at a particular site. Amateur observers can contribute much to this effort.

## Checklist of Dragonflies & Damselflies in the Victoria Region

Order Odonata
    Suborder Zygoptera – Damselflies
        Family Lestidae –Spreadwings – 5 Species

| | |
|---|---|
| Emerald Spreadwing | *Lestes dryas* |
| Lyre-tipped Spreadwing | *Lestes unguiculatus* |
| Northern Spreadwing | *Lestes disjunctus* |
| Spotted Spreadwing | *Lestes congener* |
| Sweetflag Spreadwing | *Lestes forcipatus* |

        Family Coenagrionidae – Pond Damsels – 7 Species

| | |
|---|---|
| Boreal Bluet | *Enallagma boreale* |
| Northern Bluet | *Enallagma annexum* |
| Tule Bluet | *Enallagma carunculatum* |
| Pacific Forktail | *Ischnura cervula* |
| Swift Forktail | *Ischnura erratica* |

Western Forktail — *Ischnura perparva*
Western Red Damsel — *Amphiagrion abbreviatum*

Suborder Anisoptera – Dragonflies
Family Aeshnidae – Darners – 11 Species

Black-tipped Darner — *Aeshna tuberculifera*
Canada Darner — *Aeshna canadensis*
Lake Darner — *Aeshna eremita*
Paddle-tailed Darner — *Aeshna palmata*
Sedge Darner — *Aeshna juncea*
Shadow Darner — *Aeshna umbrosa*
Variable Darner — *Aeshna interrupta*
Zigzag Darner — *Aeshna sitchensis*
Blue-eyed Darner — *Rhionaeschna multicolor*
California Darner — *Rhionaeschna californica*
Common Green Darner — *Anax junius*

Family Cordulegastridae – Spiketails – 1 Species

Pacific Spiketail — *Cordulegaster dorsalis*

Family Corduliidae – Emeralds – 5 Species

American Emerald — *Cordulia shurtleffii*
Mountain Emerald — *Somatochlora semicircularis*
Ocellated Emerald — *Somatochlora minor*
Ringed Emerald — *Somatochlora albicincta*
Spiny Baskettail — *Epitheca spinigera*

Family Libellulidae – Skimmers – 20 Species

Blue Dasher — *Pachydiplax longipennis*
Western Pondhawk — *Erythemis collocata*
Chalk-fronted Corporal — *Ladona julia*
Common Whitetail — *Plathemis lydia*
Eight-spotted Skimmer — *Libellula forensis*
Four-spotted Skimmer — *Libellula quadrimaculata*
Belted Whiteface — *Leucorrhinia proxima*
Crimson-ringed Whiteface — *Leucorrhinia glacialis*
Dot-tailed Whiteface — *Leucorrhinia intacta*
Hudsonian Whiteface — *Leucorrhinia hudsonica*
Autumn Meadowhawk — *Sympetrum vicinum*
Black Meadowhawk — *Sympetrum danae*
Cardinal Meadowhawk — *Sympetrum illotum*
Red-veined Meadowhawk — *Sympetrum madidum*
Saffron-winged Meadowhawk — *Sympetrum costiferum*
Striped Meadowhawk — *Sympetrum pallipes*
Variegated Meadowhawk — *Sympetrum corruptum*
White-faced Meadowhawk — *Sympetrum obtrusum*
Spot-winged Glider — *Pantala hymenaea*
Black Saddlebags — *Tramea lacerata*

A dragonfly up close.

# Fungi

## Bryce Kendrick

## What are Fungi?

Most people have a fairly vague idea of what fungi are, involving mush-rooms and toadstools, bracket or shelf fungi, puffballs, stinkhorns – bring-ing to mind a variety of outlandish shapes and sizes. But these are just the reproductive bodies, programmed to release large numbers of microscopic spores. Many people are unaware that moulds in houses and on food, the so-called athlete's foot, ringworm, and the rust and smut diseases that at-tack plants, are also fungi – all members of the Eumycota kingdom.

### What is a fungal individual?

Most mushrooms are short-lived local expressions of an extensive perennial network of threads, the mycelium, that lives in soil or rotting wood. Some species can extend over large areas, persist for thousands of years and pro-duce mushrooms sporadically over the entire range. The largest individual fungus yet mapped is a "colony" of a mushroom called *Armillaria ostoyae* in Oregon – it covers 900 hectares and is estimated to be 2,400 years old. This places the so-called "humungous fungus" among the world's largest organisms. So when you see a mushroom, let it expand your mind, but in a completely rational way.

### Where are fungi?

Out of sight, out of mind. Most of the time fungi are invisible, lurking as microscopic spores or as tiny branching threads in soil, wood and other substrates. Fungal threads grow only at their tips, and only there can they produce enzymes and absorb food. So the fungi always surprise us when they make their presence known. Mycologists – people who study fungi – have so far described about 100,000 species, but we are sure that more than a million still remain to be discovered.

*Amarillaria ostoyae* (left) and cup fungi (facing page).

Fungi are everywhere. They are vital components of the biosphere, for many reasons. Saprobic fungi use the remains of plants or other organisms as food – they may be the most important recyclers on the planet. Other fungi establish mycorrhizal (mutually beneficial) associations with the roots of almost all plants, passing scarce inorganic nutrients, like phosphorus, to the plant in exchange for sugars. It is no exaggeration to suggest that the land plants owe much of their success to their fungal partners. But then there are the parasitic fungi, such as rust and smut fungi, that attack plants and even other fungi.

## What is a mushroom?

A mushroom is the part of the fungal life-cycle that has to do with sexual reproduction. The extensive surface of the gills or tubes or teeth is covered with cells that produce and discharge spores – microscopic equivalents of seeds – which can travel through the air and start a new fungal colony some-where else. Mushrooms release astronomical numbers of spores, but only a few of them will survive. The mycelium, that hidden network of threads, keeps growing year after year, producing mushrooms whenever enough food has been stored, and when conditions are favourable. Some people ex-tend the term mushroom to cover other macroscopic fungi such as morels and various cup fungi.

# Which Fungi Live in the Victoria Region?

Surveys of macrofungi (those big enough to see with the naked eye) have been done for areas such as John Dean Provincial Park and Observatory Hill. Because these places are still relatively undisturbed and largely covered with forest, they are good places to look for fungal diversity.

Forests are full of fungi. All trees have some kind of mycorrhizal as-sociation with fungi, and trees tend to contribute lots of plant debris to the

forest floor, from trunks to twigs, on which the saprobic fungi thrive. Most of the mushrooms collected from Dean Park and Observatory Hill are mycorrhizal, and the rest saprobic; there were very few parasitic species.

If you want to identify macrofungi, you will need a field guide. A few of the better guides are *Mushrooms Demystified* by David Arora, *Mushrooms of the Pacific Northwest* by Steve Trudell and Joe Ammirati, and *Matchmaker*, a database program by Ian Gibson (see Kendrick in Additional Reading at the back of this book). *MatchMaker* has excellent photographs of most species and has a general identification key. It is almost essential to join some kind of local society dedicated to fungi. In the Victoria area there is the South Vancouver Island Mycological Society (SVIMS), which holds regular meetings and field trips, and will take beginners under its wing, whether they are interested in mushrooms for eating, or for aesthetic or scientific study. Enthusiasts will even teach you how to grow some edible species in your basement or yard. Search the Internet for "SVIMS" for more information.

The larger fungi can be divided into two major groups, called ascomycetes and basidiomycetes. The essential differences between these groups are actually microscopic, but in most cases the spore-producing bodies of species in one group look rather different from those in the other. The ascomycetes include the spring cup fungi (which in many cases might be better named saucer fungi), earth tongues, morels, false morels and the saddle fungi. The much more numerous basidiomycetes include: the mushrooms, which have gills (radiating vertical plates of fertile tissue); the boletes, which have vertical fleshy tubes lined with spore-producing cells; the bracket or shelf fungi or conks, usually corky or woody, growing on trees, with spore-bearing cells lining tubes; the resupinate or "spread out" fungi, usually fruiting in thin layers on the surface of dead wood; the puffballs (including earthstars), which have huge numbers of dry spores in a swollen head; the bird's-nest fungi, which make egg-shaped packets of spores in little nest-like fructifications; and the stinkhorns, which embed their spores

Puffballs.

in evil-smelling slime. Unfortunately, I do not have the space here to illustrate all of these kinds of fungi, but the books named above do it well.

Microscopic fungi also make their presence felt: when fresh peaches or cherries suddenly go brown and mushy, or when bread develops green and black spots, moulds are responsible. But we should not blame them, because they are just doing their job of recycling plant matter, though sometimes it seems they get a bit ahead of themselves. The whitish powdery coatings on leaves (especially those of squash plants, Bigleaf Maple and grasses) are also full-fledged fungi. These are called powdery mildews, and the white powder is a mass of spores. The large black spots that appear on leaves of many rose varieties (though not rugosas) are another parasitic fungus.

Ergot fungus, *Claviceps purpurea.*

The orange patches that appear on leaves of wild roses, grasses, poplars and hollyhocks, to name but a few, are produced by parasitic rust fungi (spores again). I am not going to go into the names of moulds, mildews or rusts, because you would need a microscope to confirm your identification. But they are all fungi. Occasionally, microscopic fungi produce macroscopic spore-bearing structures, as does *Claviceps*, the ergot fungus, when the fungus itself replaces the grains of its host grasses.

*Fomitopsis pinicola*, a shelf fungus.

## How many macroscopic fungi occur near Victoria?

Oluna Ceska has spent several years surveying the macrofungi of Observatory Hill (224 metres high, also known as Little Saanich Mountain) just north of Victoria, a largely forested area of about 71 hectares. She has recorded more than 1000 species so far. This is undoubtedly the most intensive macrofungal inventory ever made in the Victoria region (and probably in the whole of British Columbia). The genera most commonly encountered are, in descending order of species richness: *Mycena*, *Galerina*, *Inocybe*, *Cortinarius*, *Clitocybe*, *Psathyrella*, *Nolanea* and *Tricholoma*. Each year she encounters a fairly large number of species she has not seen before, and it would appear from studies done elsewhere that this incremental growth of the list would continue for many years. Ceska feels that she now has a good representation of the fungal community inhabiting Douglas-fir ecosystems. Undoubtedly, many different species would emerge from ecosystems dominated by other trees. Ian Gibson has compiled approximately 1850 species of macrofungi that have been recorded from Vancouver Island in his *MatchMaker* database.

Each year in October the Cascade Mycological Society holds its annual mushroom fair at the Mount Pisgah Arboretum just outside Eugene, Oregon. The fair is an exciting survey of the larger fungi because more than 300 species are usually on display – bespeaking a huge effort on the part of many members. As a guest speaker there a few years ago I was fortunate enough to obtain the statistics for fairs held over a period of sixteen years. Almost 700 species had been recorded during those years. When I arranged the data according to the number of years in which each species had been collected, an interesting picture emerged.

Only 37 species (5.5% of the total number) had been found in all sixteen years. And no fewer than 190 species (almost 30% of the total) had been recorded only *once* in those 16 years (and almost 100 more (nearly 14%) in only *two* of the 16 years). Here is the list of species totals versus years recorded.

| Species | Years recorded | Per cent of total species |
|---|---|---|
| 37 | 16 | 5.5 |
| 44 | 15 | 6.5 |
| 31 | 14 | 4.6 |
| 24 | 13 | 3.6 |
| 20 | 12 | 3.0 |
| 13 | 11 | 1.9 |
| 18 | 10 | 2.7 |
| 18 | 9 | 2.7 |
| 22 | 8 | 3.3 |
| 22 | 7 | 3.3 |
| 22 | 6 | 3.3 |
| 41 | 5 | 6.1 |
| 29 | 4 | 4.3 |
| 48 | 3 | 7.1 |
| 92 | 2 | 13.7 |
| 190 | 1 | 28.3 |

The trends are obvious: a relatively small number of species shows up every year or almost every year, a larger number is found much less often, and a very large number is encountered only once every decade or so. Forty per cent were collected only once or twice in 16 years. How many more species will show up in the years to come? What is the full number of species that the Cascade group can expect to find if they keep at it long enough? We might speculate that after 50 years they will have found 1,000 species fruiting. And we could extrapolate these data and this forecast to southern Vancouver Island with some confidence.

## When are fungi visible?

You will already have noted that the Cascade Mycological Society holds its mushroom fair in October, which is also when our local show occurs. If you move down to San Francisco, mushroom shows are held in December, while in Los Angeles they happen in January. The timing has to do with moisture and temperature. In many parts of North America and Europe mushrooms fruit mainly in the fall, with a less intense emergence in the spring. Summer and winter tend to be mushroom deserts (though there are a few hardy species, and the fruit bodies of bracket or shelf fungi are often

Fungi growing in the Victoria region (clockwise from top left): *Lycoperdon perlatum*; *Morchella angusticeps*, an edible morel; the toxic *Amanita pantherina*; *Helvella lacunosa*, a saddle fungus; a King Bolete, *Boletus edulis*; and *Amanita muscaria*, also toxic, but famous in fairy stories.

Shaggy Manes, *Coprinus comatus*.

perennial). In the Victoria area this seasonality is not nearly as obvious. Here, we can collect macrofungi in most months of the year. The fewest fungi are seen in July and August, since these months are usually dry. If mushroom mycelia are to emerge from the soil and develop fruiting bodies they need some encouragement in the form of moisture, normally supplied as rain. They also prefer temperatures above freezing, and southern Vancouver Island meets this requirement almost year round. But September and October are usually the peak season, after the fall rains begin.

## How long do the fruit bodies of fungi persist?

There is no single answer to this question. Some bracket fungi persist for years, dropping spores seasonally, and adding a new layer of pores each year. At the other end of the scale some ephemeral species of *Coprinus* shoot up overnight, quickly drop their spores, and disintegrate the next day. Between those extremes are the rest of the mushrooms, persisting for days, weeks or, occasionally, months.

# Edible or Poisonous?

I do not understand why so many of the people who pay attention to macrofungi seem driven to eat them. Certainly this does not happen with plants or most other groups of organisms. But since many people insist on eating mushrooms I must pay attention to this issue. First, most fungi are not poisonous, but neither are they worth eating. There are a few really toxic species and a relatively small number considered edible and choice. Unfortunately, there are no easy rules for distinguishing toxic and edible mushrooms. The only way to be sure is to know the fungi intimately and to be able to apply the proper (Latin) name to the species that interest you.

There are widespread beliefs that all species of the genus *Agaricus* are edible, while species of *Amanita* are toxic. Neither of these beliefs is true. There are a number of innocent-looking but unpleasant species of *Agaricus* around Victoria, and there are some good edible species of *Amanita*. But I do not have the space here to tell you which are which. As I said earlier, you will have to do a lot of homework before you can be sure, or you will have to trust implicitly in other peoples' expertise. Better not to take a chance.

## Which mushrooms are poisonous?

The most infamous of all toxic mushrooms, *Amanita phalloides*, the Death Cap, was known to occur in California, but had never been recorded here until 1998, when three specimens were found in Victoria under beech trees. This extremely toxic species has been found here on many occasions since then, often under hornbeam trees. It seems likely that it came from California with these imported non-native garden trees.

In a typical year about 70 cases of human mushroom poisoning and 30 cases of animal poisoning are reported to the North American Mycological Association for the whole continent. Poison control centres receive about 10 times this number of calls, but the vast majority involve situations where there are no symptoms – usually when a child was seen looking at a mushroom or handling it and the parents have gone into a state of panic. Only about 1 out of every 200 calls made to poison control centres is about mushrooms.

Death Caps,
*Amanita phalloides*.

Of the people actually made sick by mushrooms, only about one in a hundred die. In most years there are no deaths, but in years when fruits are abundant there can be several. This averages out to about one death per year from eating deadly mushrooms and one death every four years from a severe allergic reaction to mushrooms.

Of all mushroom fatalities, 80% are the result of eating an *Amanita* in the Destroying Angel group. *Amanita phalloides* is the member of this group eaten most frequently, causing 37% of the Destroying Angel poisoning incidents. Yet only 4% of the people who eat enough of this mushroom to get ill will die; 50% will suffer from liver damage and 6% will experience kidney failure. Symptoms typically become evident in 6 to 11 hours, but may be delayed for up to 24 hours. Getting medical help as soon as you start to feel ill really improves your chance of survival.

*Amanita virosa* and the highly similar *Amanita verna* cause liver damage in 20% of recorded cases, kidney failure in 11% and death in about 9%. Reported poisonings by *Amanita smithiana* average one every two years; kidney failure occurs in 75% of reported cases 6 to 11 hours after consumption, but none, so far, have resulted in death. Most incidents involved mistaking *A. smithiana* for a Matsutake (*Tricholoma magnivelare*).

*Amanita ocreata* appears to be the most toxic member of the Destroying Angel group. Only nine people have been poisoned in 30 years of record keeping, but liver damage was 100%, kidney failure 80% and death 40%. In humans and dogs, nursing mothers can pass *Amanita* toxins to their babies through their milk.

To spot a Destroying Angel, look for white gills and a white spore print, a cup-like sheath at the base of the stalk, and a ring on the stalk. The problem is that handling can easily obliterate the ring, and the sheath is below the ground surface and often missed. The resemblance to the choice edible Paddy Straw mushroom of Asia is striking, though Paddy Straws do not grow here. There are some edible species of *Amanita*, and some people mistake poisonous *Amanitas* for the edible ones.

## Which mushrooms are edible?

Most mushrooms are edible, and we'll look at a few of the edible and choice mushrooms. How can you recognize them? There are *no* simple ways of distinguishing between the edible and the poisonous: all folkloric tests for edibility – "If the cap peels...", "If it doesn't blacken a silver spoon...", "If the snails eat it..." – are misleading and dangerous fictions. You must *know* the name of the fungus with considerable precision before you eat it. And even then, take only a small amount the first time you eat it, in case it provokes an allergic reaction. And be aware that you can become allergic to any fungus at any time: it's a lottery. Also note that mushrooms are largely made of chitin, an indigestible polymer that also forms the exoskeletons of insects and crabs.

Pine Mushrooms, *Tricholoma magnivelare*.

Please note, before you go out looking for mushrooms, that it is illegal to pick them in any of Victoria's parks.

We can divide edible mushrooms between those that have been cultivated and those that are not or so far cannot be grown in culture. For many people, nothing matches the morels, various species of *Morchella*, that fruit in April and May. Morels often fruit profusely after forest fires. There is only one other group of ascomycetes that can compete with the morel for human attention – the truffles, various species of *Tuber*, which produce their fruiting bodies underground. Morels are found in many places on Vancouver Island, but so far, truffles have proved elusive. Morels are being grown on a relatively small scale in the USA (they are apparently rather finicky), but don't look for them in local supermarkets.

The Pine Mushroom, *Tricholoma magnivelare*, which is widely and often commercially collected, cannot be cultivated because it is a mycorrhizal species that must be associated with a living tree, as are the chanterelles (*Cantharellus* spp.). Both of these mushrooms are found near Victoria, though perhaps nowhere in British Columbia do chanterelles grow in such profusion as at Skidegate Lake in the Queen Charlottes, where many thousands of kilograms are harvested each year in early fall. There is not a great deal of research about the possible impact of collecting on the future prospects for mushrooms, but studies of chanterelles seem to show that removal of the fruiting bodies does not compromise the future of the species. This must be one of the few optimistic statements to emerge from our continuous stripping of global biological resources.

Chanterelles, *Cantherellus formosus*.

The effects on soil mushrooms of the clearcutting of forests are not so benign. One of my students determined that many mycorrhizal fungi would not return for 30 to 40 years, even after the forest began to re-grow. Removal of the trees kills the roots to which symbiotic fungi are attached and denies them the food they need. It also leaves the soil bare, so the effects of drying out, excessive heating in summer and freezing in winter can damage what fungi survive the loss of the trees.

Warning: Do *not* eat *any* uncooked mushrooms, because they contain several possible carcinogens, such as 4-(hydroxymethyl)-benzenediazonium ion and agaritine (a derivative of methylphenylhydrazine). Both of these substances break down during cooking. More insidiously, many mushrooms accumulate heavy metals from the soil, and these are *not* removed by any method of preparation or cooking. A simple rule is: don't eat mushrooms often and never eat a lot of them.

Here's a list of a few more commonly eaten species. Saprobic fungi grown on a large scale in culture include *Agaricus brunnescens* (the supermarket mushroom), species of *Pleurotus* (oyster mushrooms) and *Lentinula edodes*, (Shiitake or Oak Mushroom). Shiitake is an ideal edible mushroom, because unlike many other agarics it contains no agaritine, does not accumulate heavy metals and apparently helps to reduce cholesterol levels in the blood. I am particularly fond of dried Shiitake, which has a smoky flavour not found in fresh specimens. It does not grow naturally on Vancouver Island. *Volvariella volvacea* (Paddy Straw) is grown in the tropics and imported to North America, where it is served in most Chinese restaurants. It does not grow here in the wild. A pale form of *Flammulina velutipes* (Enoki-take), which produces very long stalks and tiny caps, is grown in culture. Most other cultivated fungi are largely eaten in Asia and do not grow here.

Fungi that cannot yet be cultivated, but are widely collected include: species of *Boletus*, especially *Boletus edulis* (known as King Bolete, Cep or Steinpilz); *Agaricus augustus* (Prince); *Lepista nuda* (Blewit); *Marasmius oreades* (Fairy Ring Mushroom); *Coprinus comatus* (Shaggy Mane), edible only when young; several species of *Armillaria* (collectively known as the Honey Mushroom, because of their colour not their taste); *Rozites caperata* (Gypsy); *Hydnum repandum* and *Hydnum umbilicatum* (Sweet Tooth or Hedgehog Mushroom – appearance, not taste); *Sparassis crispa* (Cauliflower Mushroom); and *Chlorophyllum rachodes* (Shaggy Parasol).

## What are the most common mushrooms in our area?

Here is a summary of common species and genera. The most common genera are represented locally by many species.

*Russula*, a genus symbiotic with tree roots, has more than 50 species on southern Vancouver Island. It is not hard to recognize, though many of the species can be difficult to identify. *Russula*s are usually fairly substantial mushrooms with a broad stalk and a wide cap that is usually flat or slightly concave, and often coloured (pink, red, purple, green, brown, etc.); it has a lot of neat white-to-cream gills and a brittle texture – the cap and stalk tend to break like chalk if you try to bend them.

*Hygrocybe* is generally less robust and more flexible than *Russula*, with a relatively narrow stalk, a cap that is often conical, widely spaced gills, and a waxy appearance and texture. It, too, is often brightly coloured, usually in reds and yellows. Local species include *Hygrocybe coccinea* and the much less common but spectacular *Hygrocybe psittacina*.

*Laccaria* is a mycorrhizal genus associated with conifers. The commonest species, *Laccaria laccata*, is variable but tends to produce brown caps with pinkish widely spaced gills and a darker stalk. *Laccaria amethysteooccidentalis* has a beautiful purplish colour.

*Russula brevipes*, a large and common species, is sometimes parasitized all over its surface by another fungus, a red ascomycete called *Hypomyces lactifluorum*, producing a phenomenon known as the Lobster Fungus.

Top to bottom:
*Hygrocybe psittacina*;
*Laccaria amethysteo-
occidentalis*; *Agaricus
augustus*, Prince (left),
*Hygrocybe punicea*
(right).

Western Grisette, *Amanita pachycolea.*   *Stropharia ambigua.*

*Mycena*, a saprobic genus of about 500 species, often produces numerous delicate fruit bodies with convex or conical caps, thin, usually translucent flesh, relatively few gills, and thin stalks. Colours can range from grey or white through yellow and pink to orange and red.

*Coprinus*, a saprobic genus, has crowded gills that characteristically melt away (autodigest) at maturity in blackish droplets. The size of the fruit body varies greatly from species to species, with some tiny and delicate ones occurring on herbivore dung, and the large *Coprinus comatus* (Shaggy Mane) in clusters on new lawns, fruiting from buried debris.

*Amanita*, a mycorrhizal genus, can be recognized by the loose patches of tissue on the cap, a ring on the stalk and a sheath around the base of the stalk. It has white spores and the gills are not attached to the top of the stalk. Common varieties include *Amanita muscaria* (well known to readers of fairy stories), *A. pantherina* and the recently introduced *A. phalloides* – all toxic, especially *A. phalloides*.

*Inocybe* (fibre head) species are hard to identify. Its smallish, often conical caps tend to be covered with radiating fibres, and it has a brown spore deposit. Species in this genus are not edible.

*Agaricus* species have pink gills that turn chocolate brown; they have a ring on the stalk, but no basal sheath. *Agaricus augustus* is a good edible mushroom with an almond odour. Most other *Agaricus* species in this area are *not* good to eat.

*Stropharia ambigua* is a very common black-spored species in woods around Victoria, and can be recognized when young by the fragments of veil hanging from the edge of the cap. Not edible.

93

*Gymnopilus spectabilis* fruits year after year, producing fairly massive mushrooms at the base of dead trees or around stumps. Not edible.

*Hydnum umbilicatum* and *Hydnum repandum* (Sweet Tooth or Hedgehog mushrooms) have a long season in our forests, running into the winter. These edible fruit bodies have downwardly directed teeth or spines on their underside, rather than gills. Species of *Hydnellum*, another tooth fungus, are also common, but they are corky or woody and distinctly inedible. They also have an unusual behaviour – growing around needles and twigs and incorporating them into the mature fruit body, rather than pushing them out of the way.

A few species of bracket or shelf fungi, also known as conks or polypores, can be found in and around Victoria. None are edible. *Fomitopsis pinicola*, the most common, appears as rounded, thick, woody fruit bodies growing out from trees (usually dead ones) and logs, often with a reddish band inside the margin and a whitish zone at the edge. Like other bracket fungi, it has a lower surface perforated with tiny pores, from which the spores drop into the surrounding air.

*Phaeolus schweinitzii* is easy to recognize. This inedible polypore grows from trees or on the ground, has an unusually soft texture, and tends to arise in concentric, overlapping clusters that have a yellow edge when young, but quickly become a dark chocolate brown.

*Cryptoporus volvatus* often occurs along dead trees or fallen logs. Its small, smooth fruit bodies are light brown and resemble freshly baked buns – but they are not edible. Unlike any other local polypore, the pore surface is hidden inside a tough membrane.

*Trametes* (*Coriolus*) *versicolor* (Turkey Tail) has many small overlapping, fan-shaped fruit bodies growing out from dead logs. They are thin, with very shallow white or cream-coloured pores and have several concentric zones of different colours on the upper surface. They are annual and not edible.

Many of the ascomycetes fruit in spring:

*Morchella* species (morels) are prime edibles, but relatively rare. Their ridged and pitted head makes them unmistakable.

*Helvella* species (Saddle fungi) have a stalk topped off with a smooth pale, brown or dark brown head that curves down at each side, in some species just like a saddle. Not edible.

*Caloscypha fulgens* (a spring cup fungus) is bright orange with a bluish tinge around the edge.

*Aleuria aurantia* (Orange Peel Fungus) is bright orange (as its common name suggests) and grows profusely along many logging roads.

*Scutellinia scutellata* (Eyelash Fungus) develops smallish orange cups on rotten wood, with trademark dark hairs all around the rim.

*Peziza* species are often wide, rather flat, relatively thin and brown. One species appears in damp basements.

Above: Young girls impressed by the size of *Gymnopilus spectabilis*.

Right: *Sweet Tooths, Hydnum umbilicatum*.

Below: Turkey Tails, *Trametes versicolor*.

*Xylaria hypoxylon.*

*Heterotextus alpinus.*

Jelly Tooth fungus, *Pseudohydnum gelatinosum*.

*Xylaria hypoxylon*, a different kind of ascomycete, grows profusely on rotting wood, producing narrow black branching fruiting bodies with whitish tips.

Among the jelly fungi fruiting on wood are three particularly common species:

*Pseudohydnum gelatinosum* (Jelly Tooth) looks rather like a small tooth fungus, but is translucent greyish-white with a rubbery texture.

*Dacrymyces palmatus* (Witches' Butter) produces irregularly shaped translucent yellow masses on rotten wood.

*Heterotextus alpinus* produces translucent yellow bell-shaped fruit bodies on rotten branches.

This sampling of local common species is just a glimpse of the varied visual feast that makes up the kingdom of the fungi. If you take a walk in the woods in fall, you will be rewarded by one beautiful surprise after another. Three people walking through John Dean Provincial Park in November 2010 found more than 170 species. Even if you don't want to put names on the species of fungi you find, after you have read this chapter you will already know more about them than most people do.

If you own, or have access to, a decent microscope, with a 40× objective, you can extend your study of fungi in many ways, not least by looking at moulds.

## What About Lichens?

Lichens are now recognized as fungi, even though they differ from most fungi in having domesticated algae that provide them with energy-rich foods. Because of this unique symbiosis, lichens can live in places where most other organisms can't survive, such as bare rock and the bark of trees. Because they must absorb their water and mineral nutrients from the rain, lichens are very sensitive to air pollution, and the fact that they do very well in southern Vancouver Island indicates that the air here is clean. Most

*Lichenomphalia umbellifera.*    *Lecanora xylophila.*

lichen fungi are ascomycetes, and their sexual fruit bodies are usually little cup fungi, as in *Lecanora xylophila* which grows on logs along the beach. But one common species involves a small mushroom, *Lichenomphalia umbellifera*. Lichens are beyond the scope of this chapter, but you can learn much more about them from a very fine book, *Lichens of North America*, a massive (though not very expensive) Canadian-American collaboration (see Brodo et al. in Additional Reading, page 213).

# Intertidal Life

## Philip Lambert

I often hear residents of Victoria returning from abroad and commenting on how they missed that smell of the ocean in the air. There are lots of cultural and scenic activities in this area, from whale watching to sailing, but it is hard to beat the simple pleasure of strolling along the shores around Victoria. Within a relatively short distance of the city you can explore everything from exposed rocky headlands to sheltered bays and sand beaches. Each habitat supports a different community of animals and plants, from completely protected shores like Patricia Bay to the rocks of Ogden Point breakwater or East Sooke Park, where creatures cope with heavy winter surf.

Just off the shores of Victoria, the nutrient-rich, low salinity water of the Strait of Georgia meets the cold, clear oceanic water of Juan de Fuca Strait. As a result, we can find marine species typical of the exposed coast as well as those normally inhabiting more sheltered waters.

Diverse subtital life fed by nutrient-rich waters.

Some of the interesting invertebrates living in the intertidal zone (clockwise from top left): Mopalia chiton, Heart Crab, White-spotted Rose Anemone, Gooseneck Barnacles and mussels, Scale Worm.

Naturalists will usually find something of interest along our shores year-round, but some times are better than others for beachcombing, and certain places are more accessible. In this chapter I will describe a few representative locations that are easy to get to. A very useful book, *Secret Beaches of Greater Victoria*, provides detailed information about beach access in this region and indicates the presence of tide-pools, gravel, rock outcrops, lichens and marine life.

# Tides and Tide Tables

Unlike birding and other land-based nature activities that can be done just about any time, the viewing and study of seashore life require a low tide to expose the greatest variety of animals and plants. On the coast of British Columbia we have two high tides and two low tides every 24 hours.

The Canadian Hydrographic Service publishes tide and current tables for Juan de Fuca Strait and the Strait of Georgia (Volume 5), available at many sporting goods stores, marinas and book stores. Most local newspapers also publish weekly tide tables for the area, and tide predictions are also available on the Internet at http://www.waterlevels.gc.ca/eng.

Look for the reference port closest to your area of interest. For example, use Victoria for beaches around the city and the Colwood-Metchosin shoreline, Fulford Harbour if you plan to visit the north end of Saanich Peninsula, and Sooke if you are going out to East Sooke Park or beyond.

Although these areas are not far apart in kilometres the low tide can differ by two hours between Victoria and North Saanich, so it is important to plan the timing of your trip. Aim to arrive at the beach about half an hour before the low tide. A tide height of 60 centimetres (2 ft) or less will provide the most worthwhile beach exposure for the greatest variety of species. Tides higher than this will expose only a few hardy animals such as barnacles and mussels. The low tides in May, June and July provide the best opportunity for beachcombing when they occur during daylight and for several days in a row. During this period, tides with a negative value often occur. This means they are lower than the mean low tides for the area. Good low tides also occur in November, December and January, but they are usually in the dark when only the most dedicated naturalists venture out with flashlights, rain gear and warm clothes.

A typical set of tide tables looks like this:

| FULFORD HARBOUR | JULY | | |
|---|---|---|---|
| Day | Time | Ht/ft | Ht/m |
| 8 Friday | 0045 | 10.6 | 3.2 |
| | 0845 | 0.5 | 0.2 |
| | 1725 | 10.5 | 3.2 |
| | 2115 | 9.5 | 2.9 |

The official tide tables use Pacific Standard Time and the 24-hour clock, so during Daylight Saving Time be sure to add one hour. This is a common source of error during the summer months. The height of the tide is given in feet and metres above the mean of the lowest tides referred to as "datum". In the example, the lowest tide is 0.5 feet or 0.2 metres at 0945 PDT (adding one hour to 0845 PST).

*A few words of caution:* When the tide reaches its lowest level, it turns immediately and begins to flood (rise again). As you follow the receding water, keep an eye on your return route. In some areas a flood tide may submerge your return route under a lot of deep, fast moving water in a short time.

Tide tables published in the United States use a datum that is 2.5 feet (0.8 m) higher than Canadian tables. To equate the two tables add 2.5 to the US values.

# Sandy and Muddy Shores

The action of the sea, now or in the past, has eroded thick deposits of clays and sands left by glaciers to create these kinds of shores. Changes in sea level over thousands of years have also affected the distribution of these materials.

Patricia Bay, on the northwest side of Saanich Peninsula, has a vast expanse of mud and sand. At a glance, a shore like this seems rather bleak and uninviting, but a closer look will reveal many kinds of marine life. To explore this intertidal zone you will need rubber boots, if you don't like wet feet (our waters stay rather cold year-round), a shovel or trowel, and a dip net (available from any aquarium shop).

In the sand you'll find common bivalves such as Horse Clams (*Tresus nuttallii*), Japanese and native Little Neck Clams (*Tapes philippinarum* and *Protothaca staminea*) and Bent Nose Clams (*Macoma nasuta*). Occasional squirts of water from siphon holes reveal their location. Unfortunately Saanich Inlet is closed to harvesting because of pollution. But the clams don't seem to mind – there are lots of them.

Bent-nose Clam.

You may see the coiled sand castings of the Pacific Lugworm (*Abarenicola pacifica*). This is only one of at least fifteen species of sand worms (or polychaetes) to be seen in this organic-rich sand. As the tide approaches its lowest point you'll encounter large areas of Common Eel-grass (*Zostera marina*), one of the few flowering plants that can grow in the sea. Eel-grass provides

Kelp Crab on eel-grass.

shelter for many kinds of animals, but some extra effort is required to see what lives there. If you wade into the grass and poke around with a dip net, or push the seaweed aside with your hands, you may see crabs such as the Dungeness Crab (*Cancer magister*), Horse Crab (*Telmessus cheiragonus*), Graceful Kelp Crab (*Pugettia gracilis*) and Kelp Crab (*Pugettia producta*). You will also find shrimp, including the Coonstripe (*Pandalus danae*) and sand shrimps (*Crangon* spp.). If you are really lucky you may spot a transparent, swimming nudibranch (*Melibe leonina*) which has a hood-like head and a tapering body with paddle-like flaps sticking out. There are also patches of Pacific Oysters (*Crassostrea gigas*), and surely the Sand Dollars (*Dendraster excentricus*) are among the most spectacular fauna here. Other protected areas like Tsehum Harbour, Saanichton Bay, and Deep Cove have sea life similar to that found in Patricia Bay.

Several other sandy areas, more exposed than Patricia Bay, have less mud and therefore less of the typical mud fauna. At low tide the Common Eel-grass beds on the outside of Esquimalt Lagoon spit (Coburg Peninsula) yield several species of small shrimps and Dungeness Crabs. Cordova Bay Beach has most of the typical sand fauna, including polychaete worms, sand fleas (amphipods), mud clams (*Macoma* spp.) and characteristic eel-grass creatures.

Witty's Lagoon Park includes Witty's Beach, most easily reached by parking at the end of Witty's Beach Road. The eroding cliffs of sediment provide a steady supply of sand to replace whatever the currents and winter storms wash away. Although there are stretches of mud and gravel, the beach

Moon Snail (above) and its collar (left).

is mostly sand occupied by communities of clams and other burrowing creatures. Moon Snails (*Euspira lewisii*) prey on other molluscs. One can often find clam shells with neatly countersunk holes drilled by these snails. They also construct an almost complete circle of sand and mucus containing their eggs. These sand collars, resembling a toilet plunger, should be left in place, undisturbed, so that on a high tide the larvae can burrow out and disperse in the currents to settle down a few days later. Here and there you will see holes marking the entrances to clam or shrimp holes. Those with a small mound of mud or sand around the opening are shrimp holes. When the tide covers them they busily excavate their burrows and dump their diggings at the entrance.

Witty's Lagoon Park has a nature house on the east side of the lagoon where you can learn more about the marine life of this area.

# Gravel Shores

When stronger waves act on shores of stony glacial drift, the surf draws the finer sediments offshore leaving mostly gravel, particularly during winter months.

Island View Beach, at the end of Island View Road off the Patricia Bay Highway north of Elk Lake, is a good example of a gravel beach exposed to wave action from the southeast. Fewer species live here due to the reduced amount of organic sediment and the grinding action of rocks and pebbles. On the gravel beach we find most of the common bivalves along with Purple Shore Crabs (*Hemigrapsus nudus*) under the stones. Acorn Barnacles (*Balanus glandula*) cling to the sides of larger rocks and above them a smaller species, *Chthamalus dalli*, sometimes called the Little Brown Barnacle. A few Blue Mussels (*Mytilus trossulus*) adhere to the protected sides of large boulders and nestled amongst these bivalves you may find pile worms, small crabs and whelks. Farther south along that beach where the cliffs rise up above the beach, a patch of boulders provides some habitat for the rocky shore animals, like encrusting sponges, Lemon Nudibranchs (*Doris montereyensis*), Plumose Anemones (*Metridium senile*) and Mottled Stars (*Evasterias troschelii*).

Whiffin Spit at the mouth of Sooke Harbour is an excellent spot for observing intertidal marine life, especially the beach on the exposed side of the spit. On a low tide of about half a metre (less than two feet), the exposed algae-covered bedrock may reveal some uncommon species: Leaf-shaped Crab (*Mimulus foliatus*); the small limpet *Fissurellidea bimaculatus*, which has a large, colourful mantle covering most of its shell; Smooth Velutina (*Velutina velutina*); the tiny (0.5 cm) limpet-shaped mollusc *Onchidella borealis*; the sea slugs *Peltodoris nobilis*, *Diaulula sandiegensis* and *Doris montereyensis*; and the large Red-beaded Anemone (*Urticina coriacea*) embedded in the gravel. Under the cobbles look for two kinds of peanut worms: *Themiste pyroides* and *Phascolosoma agassizii*. Compound sea squirts, small white aggregating sea cucumbers and encrusting sponges may occur around the bases of Scouler's Surf-grass) (*Phyllospadix scouleri*) at lower tides.

Plumose Anemones.

# Rocky Shores

Rocky shores often face the most vigorous waves and the strongest currents, but the myriad of cavities, cracks and crevices provide protected surfaces for more sorts of marine animals than other kinds of shores. The conditions also require you to take special care to avoid damaging the attached life and to ensure your own safety.

Cadboro Point, a rocky headland east of the entrance to Cadboro Bay, is exposed to southeast winds and strong tidal currents surging between it and Chatham Island. Ten Mile Point is a bit farther round to the north and is a favourite place for scuba divers to observe fauna typical of high-current areas. The small rocky coves of Cadboro Point are a convenient place to see rocky-shore creatures. The islets at the very tip have been declared an Ecological Reserve to protect the flora and fauna from indiscriminate collecting. A special permit from the Ecological Reserves, BC Parks, is required to do any collecting, and only for approved scientific purposes.

On the solid rock slopes you will see several kinds of barnacles. The large Thatched Barnacle (*Semibalanus cariosus*) abounds in the lower intertidal zone. Several species of limpets, from the small Finger Limpet (*Collisella digitalis*) in the upper zone to the large, flat Plate Limpet (*Notoacmaea scutum*) nearer the low-water mark graze on thin films of algae. Mixed in among these barnacles and limpets are small black Periwinkle Snails (*Littorina scutulata*) in cracks and crevices. On the lower rocks spongy mats covered with sand and bits of shell fill many of the depressions. When covered with water these mats reveal themselves as colonies of pink tentacled Aggregated Anemones (*Anthopleura elegantissima*).

Where the shore levels out and becomes a mixture of shells, rocks and small boulders we find a different community of animals. Underneath small rocks, flat-bodied Porcelain Crabs (*Petrolisthes eriomerus*), robust Red Rock Crabs (*Cancer productus*) and all sorts of hermit crabs (*Pagurus* spp.) come

Lined Chiton.

Aggregated Anemones.

scurrying out when disturbed. The underside of the rocks may be covered with layers of sponges, sea squirts or the Lined and Mossy chitons (*Tonicella lineata* and *Mopalia muscosa*). Closer to zero tide you may see Orange Sea Cucumbers (*Cucumaria miniata*) or White Sea Cucumbers (*Eupentacta quinquesemita*) in crevices or underneath rocks. The Gumboot Chiton (*Cryptochiton stelleri*) occurs on smooth rock surfaces and looks like a reddish oval dome. It may be up to 25 cm (10 in.) long, and its eight shells are covered by a leathery skin.

If you want to find unusual things, don't be afraid to get your hands wet and your knees dirty. Many of the uncommon creatures are found under rocks and ledges, or amid slippery seaweed. Take care not to crush these animals and remember to *return rocks to their original positions* so that attached creatures will not perish.

Many kinds of seaweeds cover the rocks in the Cadboro Point area, from bladderwracks (*Fucus* spp.) in the upper zone to Sea Cabbage (*Hedophyllum sessile*) in the middle to the leafy brown kelps (*Laminaria* spp.) at about zero tide. And rafts of Bull Kelp (*Nereocystis luetkeana*) float just off shore.

Ogden Point Breakwater, at the entrance to Victoria Harbour, consists of large granite blocks on the outside and broken rock on the sheltered side. This has long been a favourite place for naturalists and scuba divers interested in marine life. On the exposed side, animals similar to those mentioned

Denizens of the rocky shore. Facing page (clockwise from top): Frilled Dogwinkles, Daisy Brittle Star, Giant Red Urchin, Northern Abalone, Leather Star.

Right: Green Sea Urchin.

for the solid rock of Cadboro Point cling to the blocks and, in addition, you can find Dog Whelks (*Nucella ostrina*), Black Chitons (*Katharina tunicata*), Leafy Hornmouths (*Ceratostoma foliatum*), Blood Stars (*Henricia leviuscula*), Purple Stars (*Pisaster ochraceus*), Giant Red Urchins (*Strongylocentrotus franciscanus*) and clusters of Goose Barnacles (*Pollicipes polymerus*), to name a few. If you are lucky you might also see Northern Abalone (*Haliotis kamtschatkana*) there.

The sheltered side of the breakwater has a different community of animals from the outside. Just below the lowest tide you may see white Plumose Anemones (*Metridium senile*) or red-and-green Dahlia Anemones (*Urticina crassicornis*). The loose rocks hide all sorts of crabs: Purple Shore Crabs, Porcelain Crabs, Hairy Crabs (*Hapalogaster mertensii*), and Graceful Kelp Crabs. Sea stars such as the Mottled Star (*Evasterias troschelii*) and the Leather Star (*Dermasterias imbricata*) prefer this protected side. If you look really carefully out near the tip of the breakwater under moveable rocks you may find some Daisy Brittle Stars (*Ophiopholis aculeata*) clinging to the underside. In the subtidal areas just below, scuba divers often see masses of brittle star legs extending up into the current to feed on the particulate matter floating by. Many kinds of snails, such as Wrinkled Whelks (*Nucella lamellosa*), beautiful Golden Top Shells (*Calliostoma annulatum*) and Keyhole Limpets (*Diodora aspera*), cling to the sides of rocky crevices.

Please note that the triangular area bounded by the Ogden Point Breakwater, Brotchie Ledge (an offshore reef with a marker) and Holland Point has been set aside by the Department of Fisheries and Oceans as a protected area, with no collecting of edible species such as abalone, octopus, lingcod, scallops or sea urchins from the intertidal zone or by scuba diving. Line fishing is allowed with a valid fishing licence, available from marinas or sporting goods outlets.

The shoreline below Dallas Road beside Beacon Hill Park consists of gravel and coarse sand with little obvious fauna. But the rocky headlands and reefs exposed at low tide have flora and fauna similar to what I described for Ogden Point. In rocky crevices, look for Orange and White sea cucumbers and the small clam Arctic Saxicave (*Hiatella arctica*). With a keen eye you might see a type of stalked jellyfish (*Haliclystus* sp.) attached to some of the leafy brown algae in tide pools.

Saxe Point Park in Esquimalt has a rocky shore and colourful subtidal flora and fauna of special interest to scuba divers, who appreciate the easy access.

Harling Point on the eastside of Gonzales Bay is accessible by Crescent Road and is a semi-exposed location where some tide pools occur on a rock platform at low tide.

Cattle Point in Uplands Park offers lots of rugged outcrops and tide pools to explore, and many species similar to those found at Cadboro Point. Look for shrimps (*Heptacarpus* spp.), Black Chitons (*Katharina tunicata*), small Six-armed Stars (*Leptasterias hexactis*), and crabs such as the Porcelain Crab, Oregon Shore Crab (*Hemigrapsus oregonensis*), Purple Shore Crab, Kelp Crab (*Pugettia producta*) and hermit crabs.

Inland from these exposed sites, McKenzie Bight on Saanich Inlet, in Gowlland Tod Provincial Park, offers typical inlet scuba diving with little or no current, relatively clear water and steep rocky shelves. The inlet reaches a maximum depth of about 235 metres (770 ft). A rough gravel road called Mark Lane runs along the shore at the end of Willis Point Road, but a gate prevents cars from getting close and parking, and turn-around space is limited. It is easier to park on Ross-Durrance Lake Road, west of its junction with Willis Point Road, and walk down the McKenzie Bight trail. As this is an old roadbed, some divers bring along a wheelbarrow to convey their gear to the water's edge. The narrow intertidal zone has species typical of a sheltered rocky shore, such as barnacles, bladderwracks and periwinkles, not quite as prolific as the exposed shore. Divers will find Boot Sponges (*Rhabdocalyptus dawsonii*), Burrowing Anemones (*Pachycerianthus fimbriatus*) on mud or gravel slopes, Quillback Rockfish (*Sebastes maliger*) and, in late summer, large aggregations of Moon Jellyfish (*Aurelia labiata*).

East Sooke Park supports typical semi-exposed flora and fauna on the rocky shores below the coast trail. Large California Mussels (*Mytilus californianus*) provide protection for other species such as Dog Whelks, Porcelain Crabs, Tar Spot Sea Cucumbers (*Cucumaria pseudocurata*) and various sea worms. In the lowest intertidal levels at East Sooke look for the Purple Sea Urchin (*Strongylocentrotus purpuratus*) in cracks and crevices and Giant Green Anemones (*Anthopleura xanthogrammica*) in surge channels and tide pools.

Moon Jellyfish (above) and Frosted Nudibranch (below).

Black Katy Chitons.

# Shores of Vancouver Island's Southwest Coast

Some of the most popular southwest coast beaches occur outside the greater Victoria area between Sooke and Port Renfrew to the west. These locations bear an increasingly heavy onslaught from the open ocean swells, with a corresponding change in the species adapted to these conditions. Users favour these locations for surfing, beach combing, and storm watching.

China Beach and French Beach provincial parks and Sombrio Beach consist mostly of sand and coarse pebbles, but they provide access to the rocky shores of adjacent headlands. California Mussel beds and their associated fauna dominate the exposed rocky shores. At low tide, pools occur at the western end of French Beach and in the sandstone outcrops along the eastern end of Sombrio Beach.

Jordan River empties into Juan de Fuca Strait through thick deposits of cobbles and gravel. These form a broad stretch of beach east of the river mouth and the cobble stones harbour many Purple Shore Crabs. There is a minimum of attached flora and fauna because of exposure to waves and the grinding action of the rocks.

Botanical Beach is now a Class A Provincial Park. It is served by a road west from the government wharf at Port Renfrew to a parking lot. From there a well-maintained trail takes visitors down to the shore and the head of the Juan de Fuca Trail. This excellent intertidal site has been studied for years and was once the site of a short-lived marine station at the turn of the 20th century. Sandstone platforms that stretch eastward from the access point have many fascinating sculptured tide-pools. The platforms and tide-

Blood Star.

pools support brown and red algae and the typical flora and fauna of the open west coast: anemones, urchins, whelks, mussels, limpets, acorn and goose barnacles, Purple Stars, Blood Stars, Sea Palms, and much more. A whole chapter, if not a book, could be written about this one location.

# Beachcombing Ethics

As with other outdoor activities, try to leave the places the way you found them. If you overturn a rock to look for specimens, always return it to its original position, being careful not to crush any animals. Organisms that normally live on top of a rock would be smothered by sediment underneath and conversely, those typically found on the underside would probably die from exposure to the sun and drying air. When digging in sand or mud always refill the holes and rebury animals you have unearthed.

If you collect animals for study, keep them alive in cold seawater and return them promptly to their proper place. A permit from the Department of Fisheries and Oceans is required to collect specimens for scientific purposes. From a conservation point of view, the best place to study marine life is in its chosen habitat.

When visiting beaches at the front of private property, remember to stay below the highest tide line if there is no fence or other boundary indication.

Colour variations of Purple Stars on a rocky shore with sea grass.

On some rocky coasts you may need to find another public access to avoid trespassing. Beach fires, where permitted by local authorities, should be kept small and below the high tide line. As with any fires, be certain these are fully extinguished.

You can help reduce the needless littering of our shorelines by reporting any particularly noticeable accumulations of garbage or taking part in annual beach clean-ups in some areas. Whatever your reasons for exploring the intertidal zones, do your part to preserve these unique and fragile environments for generations to come.

Purple Sponge.

Nevertheless, accidental discoveries of ice-age mammal bones, mostly from gravel pits on the Saanich Peninsula, are evidence that an assemblage of impressive "mega" mammals roamed the Victoria area during the last ice age.

The species listed in Table 1 disappeared from North America 10,000 to 11,000 years ago, part of a wave of mammal extinctions that occurred at the end of last ice age. It is difficult to reconcile with our present ecosystems huge mammoths standing nearly five metres at the shoulder, the Short-faced Bear being larger than the modern Grizzly Bear, and herds of bison and horses. The mammoths, bison and horses were likely associated with a tundra parkland or grassland environment. The American Mastodon and Helmeted Muskox were browsers associated with forested habitats. Most of these fossils have not been dated by modern radiometric methods but based on their geological association they are assumed to date from the late Pleistocene some 18,000-25,000 years ago. One of the few dated vertebrate remains from this period is a mammoth bone from the Saanich Peninsula, radiocarbon dated at 17,000 years ago, a time when ice was beginning to advance over the area. The mammal fauna of this late pre-glacial period would have also included some of the modern species that inhabit the region today.

At full glaciation 15,000 years ago, mammals would have disappeared from Vancouver Island, surviving in areas south of the continental ice sheets or possibly in a coastal ice-free area known as a refugium, and subsequently returning as the glaciers retreated. Precisely how they reached the island after glaciation, however, is speculation. A rise in sea levels along the southeast coast of Vancouver Island following the last ice age suggests there were no land connections to the mainland. But they could have crossed to the island on ice bridges or fans of glacial outwash. A few likely swam or were carried passively on rafts of floating trees or logs; bats simply flew from the mainland. With a skimpy fossil record for the early postglacial period, we know little about when different mammal species re-colonized. The now extinct Bison evidently returned (Table 1) and survived for a few thousand years before its final demise. Bison skulls and skeletons dating from around 12,000 years ago have been recovered in several bogs and lakes on the Saanich Peninsula. The modern mammals also likely arrived in this early postglacial period. Nearly a third of Vancouver Island's land mammals are recognized as distinct races or subspecies, suggesting a long period of isolation from their mainland relatives.

*Bison antiquus* fossil skull.

## Table 2. Land Mammals of Vancouver Island.

| Common Name | Scientific Name | Present in Victoria Region |
|---|---|---|
| **Shrews – 3 native species** | | |
| American Water Shrew | *Sorex palustris* | Yes |
| Dusky Shrew | *Sorex monticolus* | Yes |
| Vagrant Shrew | *Sorex vagrans* | Yes |
| **Bats – 10 native species** | | |
| Big Brown Bat | *Eptesicus fuscus* | Yes |
| Californian Myotis | *Myotis californicus* | Yes |
| Hoary Bat | *Lasiurus cinereus* | Yes |
| Keen's Myotis | *Myotis keenii* | Yes |
| Little Brown Myotis | *Myotis lucifugus* | Yes |
| Long-eared Myotis | *Myotis evotis* | Yes |
| Long-legged Myotis | *Myotis volans* | Yes |
| Silver-haired Bat | *Lasionycteris noctivagans* | Yes |
| Townsend's Big-eared Bat | *Corynorhinus townsendii* | Yes |
| Yuma Myotis | *Myotis yumanensis* | Yes |
| **Lagomorphs – 2 introduced (I) species** | | |
| European Rabbit (I) | *Oryctolagus cuniculus* | Yes |
| Eastern Cottontail (I) | *Sylvilagus floridanus* | Yes |
| **Rodents – 6 native species, 5 introduced (I) species** | | |
| American Beaver | *Castor canadensis* | Yes |
| Black or Roof Rat (I) | *Rattus rattus* | Yes |
| Common Muskrat (I) | *Ondatra zibethicus* | Yes |
| Deer Mouse | *Peromyscus maniculatus* | Yes |
| Eastern Grey Squirrel (I) | *Sciurus carolinensis* | Yes |
| House Mouse (I) | *Mus musculus* | Yes |
| Keen's Mouse | *Peromyscus keeni* | No? |
| Norway or Brown Rat (I) | *Rattus norvegicus* | Yes |
| Red Squirrel | *Tamiasciurus hudsonicus* | Yes |
| Townsend's Vole | *Microtus townsendii* | Yes |
| Vancouver Island Marmot | *Marmota vancouverensis* | No |
| **Carnivores – 9 native species, 1 introduced (I) species** | | |
| American Black Bear | *Ursus americanus* | Yes |
| American Marten | *Martes americana* | Yes |
| American Mink | *Neovison vison* | Yes |
| Cougar | *Puma concolor* | Yes |
| Domestic Cat (I) | *Felis catus* | Yes |
| Ermine | *Mustela erminea* | Yes |

| Common Name | Scientific Name | Present in Victoria Region |
|---|---|---|
| **Carnivores (cont.)** | | |
| Grey Wolf | *Canis lupus* | Yes |
| River Otter | *Lontra canadensis* | Yes |
| Raccoon | *Procyon lotor* | Yes |
| Wolverine* | *Gulo gulo* | No |
| **Hoofed Mammals – 2 native species, 1 introduced (I) species** | | |
| Elk | *Cervus elaphus* | Yes |
| Fallow Deer (I) | *Dama dama* | Yes |
| Black-tailed Deer | *Odocoileus hemionus* | Yes |

\* Believed to be recently extirpated.

# Modern Land Mammals

Of the 30 land mammals native to Vancouver Island, 27 occur in the Victoria region (Table 2). Another 9 species are aliens introduced either accidentally or deliberately by humans. Bats account for a third of the native land mammal species on the island – not surprising, because bats can fly over the water gaps that separate Vancouver Island from the mainland. Carnivores are another dominant mammal group, with 8 native species. In contrast, the shrews and rodents are underrepresented in comparison to the mainland. Why the island's fauna is rich in carnivore species but poor in rodents is unclear, but it is a pattern evident on most of the larger islands of coastal British Columbia and Alaska.

## Shrews

Three shrews occur in the Victoria region. The largest and most specialized of these small animals is the American Water Shrew. A semi-aquatic shrew that dives under water, it lives in close association with stream-side habitats and wetlands. A stiff fringe of hairs on its hind feet acts as webbing to assist

Dusky Shrew eating an earthworm.

with swimming. A recent survey with special pitfall traps revealed that this shrew is rarely captured more than one metre from water. Its precise distribution in watersheds of the Victoria region, however, is largely unknown. There is a historical museum specimen from Millstream dating from 1897. A few individuals were captured at Veitch Creek, Niagara Creek and Rithet Creek during a survey in 1997.

The Vagrant Shrew and Dusky Shrew are generalists associated with a broad range of habitats. The Vagrant Shrew appears to be the most common and widespread shrew in the Victoria region, inhabiting forests, grassy meadows and wetlands. It is the only shrew found on the Gulf Islands. The Dusky Shrew is more closely tied to forested habitats than the Vagrant Shrew.

## Bats

Vancouver Island's 10 bat species all inhabit the Victoria region, but we know little about their distributions in the area. Except for a study in the Rocky Point Department of National Defence (DND) lands, information on the bat fauna of the Victoria region is based mostly on historical museum records, opportunistic observations of bat roosts, especially in buildings or other human-made structures, and a few captures or acoustic detections with bat detectors.

Six are small *Myotis* species. The most common are the Yuma Myotis and Little Brown Myotis. Females of both species frequently roost in buildings, such as the attics of houses, during summer. These maternity roosts, where females give birth and nurse their young, can be large, containing 1,000 or more bats. Based on my experience examining bat colonies in buildings over the years, it appears that the Yuma Myotis is the bat usually encountered in buildings on the south coast. It is also the most common bat found foraging over streams and wetlands in the Victoria region. Although we associate the Little Brown Myotis and Yuma Myotis with human struc-

Little Brown Myotis.

tures, these species also roost in trees. Small maternity colonies of the Yuma Myotis, for example, have been found in large hollows of Western Redcedar trees in the Capital Regional District parks.

Our other Myotis bats include the California Myotis, Long-legged Myotis, Long-eared Myotis and Keen's Myotis. Less is known about their biology on the south coast but the Californian Myotis and Long-legged Myotis roost in trees and are less commonly found in buildings. Keen's Myotis and the Long-eared Myotis are long-eared bats adapted for flying in cluttered forest environments and capturing insects and other prey, such as spiders, on foliage. Distinguishing these two bats is a challenge even for bat experts. Other than a few historical museum specimens of the Long-eared Myotis from Victoria and several Keen's Myotis that were captured by a cat near East Sooke Regional Park, we know little about these two bats in the Victoria region.

Larger than the Myotis species, the Big Brown Bat is occasionally found in buildings such as barns and old houses. Generally, it forms smaller maternity colonies than the Myotis bats, and it tends to use cooler, more exposed sites. This bat is also known to roost in trees and rock crevices. A rare bat in the Victoria region is Townsend's Big-eared Bat. Although it has been found roosting in large tree cavities in California, most known maternity roosts on southern Vancouver Island are in barns and the attics of houses. A small maternity colony at Mary Hill (DND site) roosts inside a World War II military structure that was associated with artillery emplacements on the hill.

Classified as tree bats, the Silver-haired Bat and Hoary Bat are rarely found in buildings, caves or rock crevices. Our largest and most striking bat, the Hoary Bat roosts in the open in branches and foliage. Although its frosted fur colour may appear conspicuous, the colour pattern actually camouflages this bat among foliage and tree branches. The Silver-haired Bat roosts under bark or in cavities in both summer and winter. Maternity colonies which may consist of several adult females and young are usually found in woodpecker cavities.

One of the mysteries of our local bats is their whereabouts in winter. No large bat hibernacula have been found on the south coast. In British Columbia's interior, most bats hibernate locally during winter, though the tree bats migrate to separate winter ranges in the United States. The only Vancouver Island bat that undergoes long distance migration to overwinter is the Hoary Bat. It has never been found here during winter. (The capture of a Hoary Bat in late September in mist nets at the Rocky Point Bird Observatory station suggests that it could migrate across the Strait of Juan de Fuca.) Although the Silver-Haired Bat is another migratory bat absent from most of Canada in winter, a winter population evidently resides in the Victoria region. There is evidence that the Californian Myotis and Silver-Haired Bat are periodically active on the coast during winter, foraging on warmer nights. In areas with cold winters, bats typically enter deep torpor or hibernation for prolonged periods in caves or abandoned mines. But in the moderate winter climate of the Victoria region where some insect prey may be available, bats likely enter short periods of hibernation and awaken to feed or drink on warmer nights.

## Lagomorphs and Rodents

No lagomorphs (hares, rabbits, pikas) are native to Vancouver Island, although the American Pika and Snowshoe Hare inhabit the coastal mainland. Of the six native rodents, four are found in the Victoria region (see Table 2). The most often seen is the Deer Mouse. Associated mostly with forested habitats, this mouse also inhabits beach and intertidal habitats. It has also managed to colonize numerous small coastal islands off Vancouver Island including the Gulf Islands. As part of an experiment in island biogeography, the Deer Mouse was deliberately transplanted to the Chatham Islands, Discovery Island, Mary Tod Island and Trial Island in Oak Bay in the early 1950s. These introduced populations likely failed to persist but their current status needs to be confirmed. Keen's Mouse, a long-tailed relative of the Deer Mouse, is found north of the Victoria region on Vancouver Island. Nearest known occurrences are Port Renfrew and the mountains near Lake Cowichan and Port Alberni. It could occur in the Sooke Hills of Victoria region, but there are no confirmed records.

The only vole on Vancouver Island, Townsend's Vole, inhabits natural open habitats with grasses or sedges: wetlands, meadows, riparian habitats, and grass balds on hill tops. Agricultural lands, such as hay fields, are also important habitat. Townsend's Vole has a spotty range on islands, absent from the Oak Bay islands but inhabiting some of the Gulf Islands. The two other rodents native to the Victoria region are the Red Squirrel, a tree squirrel associated with coniferous forests and the American Beaver, an aquatic rodent that inhabits wetlands, ponds and lakes. Although the range map in the 2007 *Peterson field guide series Mammals of North America* shows Townsend's Chipmunk on southern Vancouver Island, there are no known populations on Vancouver Island.

Two introduced lagomorphs – European Rabbit and Eastern Cottontail – have established feral populations in the Victoria region. The largest local populations of European Rabbits inhabited the grounds of the University of Victoria and the Victoria General Hospital. They seemed to be maintained by the continuing release of unwanted pets. Recent culls and live trapping removals have largely eliminated these populations. At one time, European Rabbits were released onto some of the Gulf Islands and islands in Oak Bay, but none survived. The Eastern Cottontail population on Vancouver Island is derived from animals from Ontario, where this species is native. They either escaped or were deliberately released from a property in Metchosin in the mid 1960s. Feral populations are now well established across most of southern Vancouver Island and there are unconfirmed reports from Saltspring Island.

Above: American
Beaver.

Right: Deer Mouse.

Below: European
Rabbit (left) and Eastern
Cottontail (right).

Five introduced rodents are established on Vancouver Island (see Table 2). Although the Common Muskrat is native to the British Columbia mainland, it was absent from the island until transplanted by the British Columbia Game Commission to the Cowichan and Comox valleys in the mid 1920s. It spread across the island, reaching the Victoria region and at least three Gulf Islands (Pender, Saltspring, Sidney). As with the Eastern Cottontail, the Eastern Grey Squirrel population on Vancouver Island originated from animals brought from Ontario that escaped in the late 1960s from a property in Metchosin. It has now spread throughout much of the Victoria region, probably assisted by humans capturing and releasing it into new unoccupied areas. It was removed from Newcastle and Sidney islands, but has been recently confirmed on Mayne Island, and there are unconfirmed reports from other Gulf Islands.

The House Mouse, Black Rat and Norway Rat are Old World rodents that likely arrived on the ships of the early fur traders and explorers. The first confirmed records in the Victoria region are historical museum specimens: Black Rat (1858, Esquimalt), Norway Rat (1895, Goldstream) and House Mouse (1889, Beacon Hill Park). Well-established feral populations exist throughout the Victoria region. These species occur on a few of the Gulf Islands and there are records from the 1950s of the Norway Rat on Discovery and Vantreight Islands in Oak Bay.

## Carnivores

Carnivores worth noting for their absence from Vancouver Island are the Coyote, Red Fox, Wolverine (recently extirpated), Striped Skunk, Western Spotted Skunk, Lynx and Bobcat. There is no established population of Grizzly Bears, although there have been several documented sightings on northern Vancouver Island in the past decade. All eight native carnivore species that inhabit Vancouver Island (see Table 2) occur in the Victoria region.

Of the four members of the weasel family found here, the smallest is the Ermine. Only a few records exist from the Sooke area and Saanich Peninsula, as well as historical museum specimens from Saltspring Island. Ermine living in the mountains of Vancouver Island, where there is permanent winter snow cover, acquire white winter fur, but lowland populations on southeastern Vancouver Island remain brown in winter. Strongly associated with forest habitats, American Martens persist outside urban areas in the Sooke Hills and the Greater Victoria Water Supply area. Our other weasels (American Mink, River Otter) are aquatic mammals associated with freshwater and marine environments. Both swim in the ocean and River Otters are often mistakenly identified as Sea Otters (see the chapter on Marine Mammals for a full account of the River Otter). The Raccoon is ubiquitous throughout the Victoria region and the Gulf Islands.

Large carnivores include the Grey Wolf, Cougar and American Black Bear. The Grey Wolf is now restricted to wild areas in the Malahat, Sooke

American Mink (above) and Cougar.

Grey Wolf.

Hills and Greater Victoria Water Supply Area. Historically, populations occurred on some of the larger Gulf Islands, but there are no resident wolves on these islands today. Curiously, a Grey Wolf was shot in 1984 on Sidney Island and a wolf first observed on Saturna Island was shot on Samuel Island in 2000. The source of these recent wolves is unknown, but they probably swam from Vancouver Island. American Black Bears have a similar distributional pattern to the Grey Wolf, inhabiting areas outside the urbanized municipalities of the Victoria region. There are no bear populations on the Gulf Islands. In contrast, Cougars are prevalent throughout the Victoria region, occasionally wandering into urban areas. In 1992, a Cougar trapped in the parkade of the Empress Hotel had to be tranquilized and removed by conservation officers. There are occasional reports from Saltspring Island, and in 2001 a Cougar was shot on James Island.

## Hoofed Mammals

Black-tailed Deer are ubiquitous throughout the Victoria region. With sparse snow cover in winter and natural predators such as the Grey Wolf and Cougar rare or absent in the more developed areas, deer thrive in the suburban and urban landscapes of Victoria, much to the chagrin of gardeners and farmers. The Capital Regional District is developing a management strategy that is intended to reduce the deer population and deer-human conflicts. Although there are occasional reports of Elk tracks and sightings, the Victoria region is largely outside the main range of this species on Vancouver Island. Most of these occurrences are likely transient animals.

Fallow Deer are found on James, Sidney and Mayne islands and there are occasional sightings on D'Arcy Island. The James and Sidney populations originated from animals transplanted from the Chatsworth Estate in England to James Island in 1908 for hunting. In the 1930s, Fallow Deer from James Island were introduced to Saltspring and Pender islands, and to the Alberni valley, but they did not survive. The population on Sidney Island is derived from animals that swam from James Island. The Mayne Island population originated from recent escapes from a Fallow Deer farm on the island. Fallow Deer tracks are seen on rare occasions on the eastern side of the Saanich Peninsula but there are no established populations on Vancouver Island.

Black-tailed Deer.

# Conservation

When the first Europeans settlers and fur traders established Fort Victoria in the 1840s they would have encountered Grey Wolves, American Black Bears, Cougars, Elk, and furbearers such as American Marten in what is now essentially downtown Victoria. These animals were pushed out of urbanized areas, but most still reside in outlying areas. Except for the Elk, no native land mammal has been extirpated from the Victoria region in historical time. The Wolverine, recently extirpated from Vancouver Island, and the endangered Vancouver Island Marmot are mammals that probably never inhabited the Victoria region in early historical time.

Ancient faunas on isolated oceanic islands such as the Galapagos and Hawaiian Islands are highly vulnerable to habitat changes or introduced species because they are over-specialized and unable to adapt. But the vertebrates of Vancouver Island are relatively recent arrivals. The island nature of Vancouver Island has tended to filter out highly specialized mammals, favouring generalists with broad habitat requirements, traits that make them good colonizers and survivors on islands. In contrast to some of the invertebrates and plants, none of our native mammals have ranges confined to the Garry Oak ecosystems of southeastern Vancouver Island, and the Victoria region represents only a small portion of their overall range on the island.

Raccoons adapt well to urban environments.

## Mammals at Risk

Of the 27 native mammals in the Victoria region, 5 are formally listed by the province (Table 3) to be of conservation concern. Two (American Water Shrew and Ermine) are subspecies restricted to Vancouver Island and associated islands. In British Columbia, the Roosevelt subspecies of Elk is also confined to Vancouver Island other than a few areas on the mainland where it was reintroduced. Only one species, the Keen's Myotis, has been assessed nationally by the Committee on the Status of Endangered Wildlife in Canada (COSEWIC). The American Water Shrew, bats and Ermine are listed because of rarity and life history traits that may make them vulnerable to disturbance or habitat loss. Despite their provincial listings, no comprehensive surveys or monitoring have been done in the Victoria region and their distribution, population trends and habitat associations are unknown.

In contrast, the Elk population on Vancouver Island has been well studied. According to a recent provincial status report, the island's population of about 3,300 animals appears to be stable. Although there are no established populations in the Victoria region today, this species was evidently common and widespread on southeastern Vancouver Island in the past. Bones dating from 500 to 1500 years ago have been recovered in archaeological sites in Oak Bay and the Fort Rodd Hill historical site, and on several of the Gulf Islands. Early Spanish explorers described Elk herds in what is now Esquimalt Harbour. Hunting, particularly by professional market hunters in the mid 1800s, probably played a role in extirpating the local Elk population.

## Table 3. Land Mammals of the Victoria Region Listed Provincially and Nationally to be of Conservation Concern.

| Common Name | Scientific Name | BC Status | COSEWIC Status |
|---|---|---|---|
| **Shrews** | | | |
| American Water Shrew, Vancouver Island subspecies | *Sorex palustris brooksi* | Red[1] | Not Assessed |
| **Bats** | | | |
| Keen's Myotis | *Myotis keenii* | Red | Data Deficient[2] |
| Townsend's Big-eared Bat | *Corynorhinus townsendii* | Blue[3] | Not Assessed |
| **Carnivores** | | | |
| Ermine, Vancouver Island subspecies | *Mustela erminea anguinae* | Blue | Not Assessed |
| **Hoofed Mammals** | | | |
| Elk, Roosevelt subspecies | *Cervus elaphus roosevelti* | Blue | Not Assessed |

1. Red = endangered or threatened in BC.
2. Insufficient biological information to rank this species.
3. Blue = vulnerable in BC.

None of these listed mammals are facing imminent extinction. Rather than concentrating on recovery strategies for the listed species and subspecies, conservation efforts need to be more holistic, directed at maintaining the region's diversity and populations of both the rare and common species.

# Threats

## Habitat Loss

In 2011 the human population in the Capital Regional District reached 376,222 – an increase of about 160% from 50 years ago. The region's population is projected to reach 425,500 by 2030. Associated with population growth are housing development, roads, shopping malls, golf courses and the inevitable loss of natural habitats and agricultural lands. A glance at historical maps or air photos reveals the scale of growth and habitat loss in the region over the past 50 years.

Some of our native mammals – such as the Raccoon and Black-tailed Deer – manage well in urban areas, but large carnivores – Grey Wolf, American Black Bear and Cougar – require extensive tracts of continuous habitat. As residential areas creep into wild areas, problems with wildlife arise, such as bears scavenging in human garbage, often resulting in the destruction of these animals.

# Table 4. Summer Roosts of Bats in the Victoria Region

| Species | Trees | Rocks & Cliffs | Buildings | Bat Houses |
|---|---|---|---|---|
| Big Brown Bat | X | X | X | X |
| Californian Myotis | X | X | X | X |
| Hoary Bat | X | | | |
| Keen's Myotis | X | X | X | |
| Little Brown Myotis | X | X | X | X |
| Long-eared Myotis | X | X | X | ? |
| Long-legged Myotis | X | X | X | X |
| Silver-Haired Bat | X | | | |
| Townsend's Big-eared Bat | ? | | X | |
| Yuma Myotis | X | X | X | X |

Development and urbanization reduce habitat for forest-dependent species. Nine of the ten bats in the Victoria region use trees as summer roosts and two species roost only in trees (Table 4). Before the arrival of humans and their structures, even the Myotis bats we now associate with buildings were heavily dependent on trees. In fact, their use of buildings may in part be attributed to a loss of suitable tree roosts. Except for the Hoary Bat, which roosts in foliage, bats prefer large, old live trees or snags with loose bark or cavities. Because they frequently change their tree roost throughout the summer, a local bat population will require a number of wildlife trees to meet its roosting needs. Protecting a few wildlife trees is not enough. Other forest-dependent mammals are the American Marten and Red Squirrel, the latter dependent on conifer cones for winter food.

Most habitat loss and deterioration in the region can be attributed to human activity. But on some of the Gulf Islands the native Black-tailed Deer populations have become abundant with the historical loss of predators such as the Grey Wolf and Cougar and the decline in human hunting. Overbrowsing by deer has reduced the shrub understorey with an associated decline in nesting songbirds.

Aquatic mammals such as the American Beaver are sensitive to the loss of wetlands and riparian habitats. The red-listed American Water Shrew is dependent on riparian habitats and streams with high water quality. Ponds, lakes and riparian habitats with their abundant flying insects are also highly productive foraging sites for bats.

Although agricultural lands, such as old fields, could be dismissed as human-made habitats, they support grassland species such as Townsend's Vole that may reach its highest densities in agricultural lands. More than 70% of the Barn Owl diet on Vancouver Island is Townsend's Vole and it is also likely the preferred food of the Ermine. Old barns or attics in old farm

130

A roost of blue-listed Townsend's Big-eared Bats.

houses provide habitat as maternity roosts for eight of our bat species (Table 4). Most of the known maternity roosts on Vancouver Island of Townsend's Big-eared Bat, for example, are in human structures. Modern buildings generally lack large attics and with modern weather sealing are usually inaccessible to bats.

A counterbalance to habitat loss is the outstanding system of parks and protected areas in the Victoria region, including five provincial parks, about thirty regional parks, the Gulf Islands National Park Reserve, and various small municipal parks. Some are too small and disconnected from other natural areas to sustain wild mammal populations, but the larger parks, such as East Sooke, Sooke Hills, Sea-to-Sea, Sooke Mountain, Gowlland Tod and Goldstream, protect significant tracts of habitat. Moreover, several are contiguous with lands of the Greater Victoria Water Supply Area, creating a network of connected wild lands. As the human population increases in the region there will be more demands for recreational access and facilities in these protected areas. Careful management, balancing preservation of biodiversity with recreation, will be critical for maintaining wildlife populations for future generations. Sound management decisions require good inventory data. Unfortunately, in contrast to the birds and rare plants, mammal inventories and monitoring programs are lacking for these protected areas.

## Introduced Mammals

With nine introduced species, about 20% of the region's mammals are aliens. All have well-established populations, are adapted to urban landscapes, and I suspect that none can now be eliminated from Vancouver Island. Some may be a threat to our native mammals, other wildlife species

131

and native plants. Remarkably, except for Fallow Deer on James and Sidney islands, there have been no inventories, monitoring or research of these alien mammals. Their impact is largely speculative.

The Eastern Grey Squirrel has been much vilified as a threat to the smaller native Red Squirrel. It has been argued that in deciduous woodlands, particularly Garry Oak habitats, the Eastern Grey Squirrel is displacing the Red Squirrel. Nevertheless, detailed information on the historical range and populations of the Red Squirrel in the Victoria region is lacking. Although the Red Squirrel has disappeared from some areas, the loss of coniferous forest tracts during development, along with predation by Domestic Cats have probably contributed more to its demise than competition with the Eastern Grey Squirrel. Of more concern is the relationship between Garry Oaks and the Eastern Grey Squirrel. The squirrel helps disperse seeds by burying acorns but it also is known to chew the ends of acorns to prevent them from germinating. Of our introduced mammals, this is the species in most urgent need of research.

Unlike the European Rabbit, which is restricted to isolated populations in the wild, the Eastern Cottontail has now spread across much of southern Vancouver Island and is an established component of the fauna. Its impact of the island's fauna has not been studied, but with no native lagomorphs it could be filling an empty niche. Research in Mill Hill Regional Park has shown that grazing by this rabbit can impact threatened native plants such as White-topped Aster.

Feral populations of the House Mouse, Black Rat and Norway Rat occur in agricultural lands, urban parks, and residential areas. Native rodents such as Townsend's Vole or Deer Mouse are often rare or absent from habitats occupied by these species, but to what extent their absence can be attributed to competition from introduced rodents or habitat changes is unclear. On the Queen Charlotte Islands, the native Keen's Mouse has disappeared from several islands where rats were introduced.

Red Squirrel.

Eastern Grey Squirrel.

## Table 5. Recent records of alien mammals in the Victoria region that failed to establish populations or have no known status.

| Name | Occurence | Status |
|------|-----------|--------|
| North American Opossum *Didelphis virginianus* | Road kills near Victoria airport and the Malahat and sightings in Cordova Bay in the 1990s. | not established |
| Yellow-bellied Marmot *Marmota flaviventris* | A single animal observed at North Saanich Marina in 2006. | not established |
| | A single animal seen on the grounds of the Empress Hotel from 2008 to 2010. | not established |
| Chipmunk unknown *Neotamias* sp. | 36 introduced to Sidney Island from Oregon in 1965. | unknown |
| Coypu *Myocastor coypus* | Animals escaped from fur farms in the 1950s and 1960s. Recent sightings on Saltspring Island. | unknown |
| Domestic Ferret *Mustela putorius* | Road kills on Patricia Bay Highway in 1990s, likely escaped pets. | not established |
| Striped Skunk *Mephitis mephitis* | Road kills and sightings on Saanich Peninsula and in Metchosin in the 1980s. | not established |
| Coast Mole *Scapanus orarius* | Trapped on University of Victoria campus in 2009. | not established |

At least seven other alien mammals have appeared in the Victoria region over the past few decades (Table 5). None are established but they demonstrate the ongoing threat posed by introductions. Most of these new arrivals were either escaped pets or animals deliberately released into the wild by humans; but the North American Opossums could have been brought accidentally in the back of a farm truck, and the Coast Mole was evidently in the root ball of a new tree.

## Other Threats

Except for mortalities from road collisions, direct killing of wildlife by humans is not a major conservation issue. Other than the early market hunting, hunters have not had a major impact on local wildlife populations; in fact, hunting groups have been strong supporters of wildlife conservation. In recent years, the number of hunters and areas offering hunting opportunities in the Victoria region has declined. In the past, bats in buildings were

133

routinely fumigated. Now, they are protected under the provincial Wildlife Act and reputable pest control companies now use exclusion techniques to eliminate bats from buildings. Domestic Cats continue to be a major source of mortality for smaller mammals. Ironically, in urban and rural agricultural areas where the native small mammalian predators are extirpated, the Domestic Cat is probably the most effective mammalian predator of introduced rabbits, rats, mice and squirrels. Unfortunately, cats also kill birds and native mammals including shrews, bats, voles, Red Squirrels and Ermine.

# What Can you Do?

## Stewardship

A first step is simply to become more tolerant of our native mammals and appreciate that we share the land with animal species that have occupied this area for thousands of years. Property owners in suburban or rural areas can make their land wildlife friendly by maintaining natural vegetation and providing ground cover with brush piles and shrubs. Unless they are a risk to buildings, do not cut down wildlife trees as they provide dens for Raccoons and roost sites for bats. Avoid the use of pesticides, because bats and shrews will pick up the pesticide residues from their invertebrate prey. Controlling Domestic Cats is a sensitive issue for cat owners, but maintaining cats on a leash or, better yet, keeping them indoors will reduce the toll on local birds and small mammals.

Except for Black-tailed Deer damaging gardens or colliding with motor vehicles and the occasional Red Squirrel or Raccoon occupying an attic, bats are the native mammals that most frequently come into conflict with humans, because of their tendency to live in human-made structures. Most bats occupying buildings in summer are female maternity colonies where the young are born and nursed. Females require warm, stable conditions during pregnancy and nursing, and for some species homes, barns and other structures provide ideal conditions. If bats are not creating a nuisance or are using unoccupied buildings such as barns, the best approach is to live with them and benefit from their insect-eating habits. They are major predators of night-flying insects, including many pest species such as mosquitoes, termites, bark beetles and moths. But when a large colony produces odours or where bats are entering human living-quarters, it may be necessary to evict the colony. The recommended approach is to exclude the bats by sealing or blocking the openings they use to enter the structure. To avoid trapping bats inside, any exclusion work should be done in autumn or winter after the bats have left the summer colony. Even closing off structures after dark in summer is risky as some adult bats and young bats unable to fly may be trapped inside. Detailed information on bats in houses and instructions for exclusion can be obtained from Bat Conservation International and the provincial Ministry of Environment.

An increasingly popular conservation activity is installing bat houses. Bat houses can be used to provide alternative roosts after bats have been evicted from a building or to attract bats for controlling insects. At least five bat species in our area (see Table 4) are known to use bat houses. In the United States, some organic farmers are using bat houses on a large scale as a biologically friendly method for controlling agricultural insect pests. Another benefit of bat houses is bat guano, which is an excellent fertilizer in the garden. To attract maternity colonies, bat houses need to be large and installed in areas with maximum sun exposure. As an example of how effective bat houses can be, eight maternity houses recently installed at a BC Hydro station near Campbell River house about 1,000 Yuma Myotis and Little Brown Myotis in summer. Excellent instructions and plans for bat houses can be obtained from Bat Conservation International.

## Record Your Observations

Birds and plants have long attracted the interest of local naturalists, but mammals have received less attention because they are difficult animals to observe in the wild. Many are secretive in their habits, limiting any observations to a brief chance encounter. Another challenge is that some mammals are active mostly at night. Identification can be intimidating. Shrews and many bats are impossible to identify unless you actually have the animal in the hand. Still, some of our diurnal mammals are easy to observe and identify in the field. Searching for tracks, particularly after one of our rare winter snow falls, and other distinctive signs, such as scats, marks on vegetation and den sites, can reveal the presence of mammals and provide insights into their local natural history.

Large, fruity scat indicates that a bear is in the area.

A small tree felled by a beaver.

A paw print in the snow reveals that a Cougar has walked this way.

For some species, we have little knowledge of distributions in the Victoria region. The field naturalist can make an important contribution by recording the date, location (including coordinates if you have a GPS device) and circumstances of mammal observations. If you have a camera, try to photograph any unusual sighting. Road kills and dead animals brought in by the cat are also a source of new information. Because of the risk of rabies, do not handle any dead bats unless you are wearing rubber gloves. Your observations should be passed on to the Ministry of Environment or the Royal BC Museum. Of particular significance are records of species outside their expected local range, of rare mammals like the American Water Shrew or Ermine, of bat colonies, and of introduced species like the Eastern Grey Squirrel and Eastern Cottontail. Watch for the appearance of new introductions, too. Recent reports of Yellow-bellied Marmots and Coast Moles are the latest records in a long list of alien mammals brought to the region. With people's tendency to release unwanted pets or transport wild animals to different areas, more surprises can be expected.

# Marine Mammals

## Anna Hall

Marine mammals, like their terrestrial relatives, are warm-blooded, breathe air, give birth to live young and produce milk. Whales, dolphins and porpoises are entirely aquatic, while otters, seals and sea lions divide their time between sea and land. To maintain a warm internal temperature, whales, dolphins and porpoises have a layer of insulating blubber, while seals, sea lions and otters have insulating fur as well as a layer of fat.

The waters around Victoria provide both seasonal and year-round habitats for the 14 species of marine mammals listed below. This chapter summarizes the natural history of each mammal and offers suggestions for possible viewing locations.

## Marine Mammals of the Victoria Region

| Common Name | Scientific Name | Occurrence |
|---|---|---|
| River Otter | *Lontra canadensis* | Common, year round |
| Sea Otter | *Enhydra lutris* | Rare |
| Harbour Seal | *Phoca vitulina* | Common, year round |
| Northern Elephant Seal | *Mirounga angustirostris* | Common, seasonal |
| Northern Fur Seal | *Callorhinus ursinus* | Rare |
| California Sea Lion | *Zalophus californianus* | Common, seasonal |
| Steller Sea Lion | *Eumetopias jubatus* | Common, seasonal |
| Harbour Porpoise | *Phocoena phocoena* | Common, year round |
| Dall's Porpoise | *Phocoenoides dalli* | Common, year round |
| Killer Whale | *Orcinus orca* | Common, seasonal |
| Pacific White-sided Dolphin | *Lagenorhynchus obliquidens* | Rare |
| Grey Whale | *Eschrichtius robustus* | Common, seasonal |
| Minke Whale | *Balaenoptera acutorostrata* | Common, seasonal |
| Humpback Whale | *Megaptera novaeangliae* | Occasional, seasonal |

# Otters

Otters belong to the weasel family (Mustelidae). Both River and Sea otters can be seen in the Victoria area, but Sea Otters only rarely. When you see an otter swimming in the ocean, it's almost certainly a River Otter.

## River Otter

River Otters are one of the more common seashore mammals of southern Vancouver Island and people often see them running on a beach to or from their terrestrial dens. A fully grown River Otter can reach almost 1.4 metres in length and weigh up to 14 kilograms. Its long tail can be more than a third of its entire body length.

This sleek, agile creature has a rich, brown fur coat, a prominent snout with coarse whiskers, pointy ears and webbed feet. It has remarkable agility on land and can run at speeds of up to 29 km/h. It's also an excellent swimmer, able to cover up to 11 km/h, but it's more difficult to observe in water, because most of its body is under the surface. A River Otter can close its nostrils and ears while diving for food and can stay under water for up to two minutes.

River Otters hunt for food on land and in the water, preying on fish, shellfish, frogs, birds and small mammals, catching their food with their mouths rather than their claws. They will also raid nests of diving birds and shorebirds to eat the eggs. They have few natural enemies in the ocean, but young otters on land are sometimes snatched up by Bald Eagles.

These highly social creatures can often be seen in groups, sometimes playing or chirping and twittering at each other. They mature by about age 3 and can live up to about 15 years. River Otters make their dens on land in natural hollows under logs or in riverbanks, in the abandoned dens of other animals, or even under a backyard deck or in a boat moored to a dock. They mate in late winter, but females can delay the implantation of their ovaries for about eight months, so they give birth in the spring of the following year to litters of up to four kits.

River Otters are often seen on the Victoria waterfront.

Habitat loss, chemical pollution and litter are threats to River Otters. Oil spills pose a great risk, because oil coats the fur and reduces its ability to insulate the animal against the cold.

You can find River Otters in any coastal or freshwater area on southern Vancouver Island. They are more active at night, but sometimes hunt or travel in daylight. If you come across their dark, odorous scat, which often contains bits of shells and fish bones (often left behind on logs, docks and boat decks), you'll likely find otters close by. Your chances of sighting one are better in the morning and early evening.

## Sea Otter

Sea Otters are rarely seen in Victoria waters and almost never on land. They have lighter brown fur than River Otters, and the head is silvery-grey to brown. Thick fur on the head makes the ears appear smaller than those of River Otters. Adult Sea Otters are only slightly longer than River Otters (up to about 1.5 metres), but are almost three times as heavy (up to 45 kg), and the tail is proportionately shorter, at about a quarter of the body length.

Unlike all other marine mammals, a Sea Otter lives almost all its life at the ocean's surface, where it swims, rests, feeds and reproduces. Its dive times are relatively short, usually less than a couple of minutes. It eats marine invertebrates, mostly sea urchins, clams, mussels, snails, abalone, octopus and crabs, catching them with its hands rather than its mouth. This species is well known for its use of tools. A Sea Otter will use a rock or another hard object (including a discarded bottle or can) to break open a shellfish. Some appear to have a favourite tool that they keep and use repeatedly.

Sea Otters are often seen floating on their back. The buoyancy of their fur is critical for survival, so they spend much of their time grooming to ensure their fur is clean and dry.

This species has the densest fur of any mammal, a quality that almost caused its demise. Commercial fur traders in the 18th and 19th centuries eradicated Sea Otters from much of British Columbia's coast. Now,

Sea Otters are gradually returning to their former ranges.

a re-introduced population on northwest Vancouver Island appears to be increasing and may converge with the northwestern Washington population.

Sea Otters can reproduce in any season, but a female mates just once a year, producing a single pup. The pup stays with its mother for five to eight months. Sea Otters are social animals and make a variety of noises for communication including squeaks, chirps, whistles and whines.

Your chances of seeing a Sea Otter in the ocean around Victoria are not good, but sightings have been recorded near Race Rocks and in the waters adjacent to the Victoria Golf Course in Oak Bay. Most were single animals, possibly young males looking to expand their territory.

# Seals and Sea Lions

Seals and sea lions belong to a group of animals known as pinnipeds (meaning "fin-footed"). Seals can be distinguished from sea lions by their lack of external ears and their small fur-covered foreflippers. Sea lions are more agile on land than seals. They can rotate their pelvic girdle so that the hind flippers help support their body weight and allow them to walk on land. Five species of pinnipeds inhabit the marine waters around Victoria throughout the year. From land, it is best to look for seals and sea lions at rest on the shore and on exposed rocks at low tide.

## Harbour Seal

Harbour Seals are the smallest and most commonly observed pinniped in the Victoria area, because they live here year round. It's easy to see them on exposed rocks along the shore. Watch for them lying with their heads and flippers held in the air, in the shape of a smile or banana.

Harbour Seals often visit docks and marinas.

Harbour Seal fur ranges in colour from light tan to black, mottled with dark and light rings and patches. As with many marine animals, the fur is usually darker on the dorsal surface (back) and lighter on the underside. While swimming at the surface, often only the round head, short muzzle and whiskers appear above water – they can look like a dog, but they do not splash while swimming.

Males grow to be slightly larger than females, but the sexes cannot be distinguished when looking at wild seals. They can reach 1.9 metres in length and weigh up to

Harbour Seals resting on shore.

about 120 kg. In the wild, males can live to about 25 years and females to about 35 years.

Females give birth on shore to single pups. In the Victoria region, the pupping season lasts from June to September, peaking in July and August. The pup is able to swim a few hours after birth and is weaned in about six weeks. Harbour Seals mate shortly after pups are born, usually in the water.

The female gives all the parental care. She will sometimes leave her pup for many hours while on foraging expeditions. If you see a healthy pup alone and think it might be abandoned, it is best to watch it from a distance for at least 24 hours. The mother will likely return. Mothers and pups locate each other by smell and sound. It is important to avoid disturbing Harbour Seals on shore and in the water, especially during the summer reproductive season.

Harbour Seals usually swim alone, but sometimes gather in large numbers while on shore. They can dive to a depth of 300 metres and adults can remain submerged for up to 25 minutes. They eat a variety of shellfish and fishes, including herring, salmon, smelt, perches and flatfishes. They also eat hake, and since hake eat juvenile salmon, removing Harbour Seals from the marine food web would likely have a negative effect on salmon populations. Transient Killer Whales and sharks are natural predators of these seals.

Until the 1960s, people hunted Harbour Seals commercially and killed them for a bounty offered by the Canadian Department of Fisheries and Oceans. These incentives contributed to a significant reduction in the population. Since the 1970s, Harbour Seals have been protected, and today the British Columbian population appears to have returned to its historic numbers, or has even surpassed it. Chemical and plastic pollution and illegal shooting still threaten this marine mammal.

Harbour Seals are commonly seen in calm marine waters around Victoria. These clever animals have learned that hanging around fish-cleaning stations at marinas can lead to an easy meal. Good places to look are Victoria's Inner Harbour, especially near Fisherman's Wharf, and Pedder Bay Marina, Esquimalt Lagoon, Oak Bay Marina and the Chain Islands.

## Northern Elephant Seal

The Northern Elephant Seal is the largest pinniped in the Victoria area. The males really are elephant-sized – they can reach 4.6 metres in length and weigh up to 2700 kg. Their bulk and large, overhanging snout distinguishes males from females and juveniles. Females reach only 3.4 metres long and a weight of 770 kg. Both sexes have short front and hind flippers, no external ears and less fur than other seals. Males are grey to brown and can have extensive white scarring on the neck.

Usually only males and juveniles are seen in our waters. But a female and newborn pup were observed at Race Rocks in January 2009. This is believed to be the first birth of a Northern Elephant Seal in this area.

Northern Elephant Seals are migratory, with breeding rookeries in California and Mexico. The breeding season runs from December to March. The males mate with many females, and about a year later the females give birth on shore to a single pup. This is why pups are rarely seen here, because they are born during the breeding season in the south. Yet some animals have been seen onshore here in winter months, even though this is not an area where this species normally breeds.

Sightings of Northern Elephant Seals have increased in recent years.

Northern Elephant Seals can live for 20 years. They spend most of their time at sea, coming ashore only for mating and moulting. Females generally moult in May and June, followed by the males in July and August. While ashore, these seals do not feed, but rely on their stored fats. During moulting, they can look sickly, with pieces of fur and skin sloughing off, and their eyes and noses weeping. Sometimes, their skin gets mildly infected, which results in bleeding, making these perfectly healthy animals look even worse. Unfortunately, in the past, people misunderstood the process and shot healthy moulting seals thinking that they were putting them out of their misery.

Before commercial hunting, this species abounded in the Pacific Ocean. But at the end of the 19th century, it was considered commercially extinct – the population might have been as low as 20 animals. Mexico was the first country to enact protection for the Northern Elephant Seal, and the few remaining animals founded the current population of more than 150,000 in the North Pacific.

Northern Elephant Seals have a varied diet that includes squid, octopuses, crabs, bottom fishes, small sharks and rays. They can spend almost all their time at sea and remain under water for more than an hour while diving to an astonishing 1250 metres deep. Sharks and Transient Killer Whales are their natural predators.

While at sea, a Northern Elephant Seal often hangs vertically in the water with just its head above the surface. In this position, it resembles a deadhead log. Usually only single animals are seen at sea, but up to a dozen will go ashore together. While lying on shore, elephant seals blend in with the colour of the rocks on southern Vancouver Island. Around Victoria, they have been seen moulting on the shores of the Gorge waterway, Ten Mile Point, and several beaches in Metchosin. Race Rocks is one of the best places to see Northern Elephant Seals during the summer months.

## Northern Fur Seal

Northern Fur Seals are rarely seen in the Victoria area. They prefer the open ocean over banks and shelves where greater quantities of fishes and other prey species live. These seals pass through British Columbian waters on their annual migrations between their summer breeding rookeries on the Pribilof Islands in the Bering Sea and their feeding areas as far south as California.

Northern Fur Seals have external ears, long front and rear flippers, and long whiskers. They generally range in colour from greyish-brown to black. At up to 270 kg and 2.1 metres in length, adult males are much larger than females, which can grow to about 50 kg and 1.5 metres. They can dive to 180 metres below the surface while hunting for fishes, crustaceans, squid and octopuses. They can live as long as 25 years.

Your best chance of seeing a Northern Fur Seal is from a boat at quite a distance from shore. At sea, they rest on their backs with their rear flippers extended over their abdomen and their head stretched back. Sealers used to call this the "jug handle" position.

Historically, this species was extensively hunted for its high-quality fur. Though the population is fairly large, at more than 600,000, it has declined significantly over the past few decades. Scientists don't know the reasons for the decline, but they do know that many fur seals have drowned from getting entangled in discarded fishing gear and other plastics.

Steller Sea Lion.

## California and Steller Sea Lions

Both California and Steller sea lions arrive in Victoria waters in the fall and stay throughout the winter and spring months. Race Rocks is one of the best places to see these two species, but they'll haul out on human-made structures, too, like docks, log booms and navigational buoys. Females are rare sights here. It's the males that come to this area, often in large groups. Watch for them during any winter ferry crossing.

Both species are large and brown, and have ears, long whiskers and furless flippers. They are agile on land and in water. Both are excellent swimmers, capable of reaching 32 km/h and diving to at least 140 metres depth.

You can distinguish these eared seals by their differences in colour, size and vocalizations. California Sea Lions have rich chocolate-brown fur and a pronounced forehead; Steller Sea Lions are lighter brown. Male California Sea Lions grow up to 2.4 metres long and weigh 300 kg (females can be 1.8 metres long and weigh 100 kg). Male Steller Sea Lions can grow to 3 metres long and weigh 900 kg (most females reach about 2 metres and weigh about 270 kg). California Sea Lions bark, whereas Steller Sea Lions growl or roar.

Steller Sea Lions breed from June to August, at rookeries along the coast. There are a few breeding rookeries in British Columbia, but none near Victoria. California Sea Lions breed in May and June at specific rookeries in southern California and northern Mexico. The females of both species stay near their rookeries year round; they nurse their pups for up to three years. After mating, the males leave and spend the rest of the year in the company of other males moving along the coast to different haul-out sites.

Steller and California sea lions.

California Sea Lions can live to about 30 years, but Steller Sea Lions just 17. Both species eat squid and octopuses, and a variety of fishes, including hake, herring, salmon, lamprey eels and anchovies. Transient Killer Whales and sharks prey upon them. Others are killed by humans and human activities, from illegal shooting and pollution to getting tangled in fishing gear or anti-predator nets at aquaculture facilities.

The population of California Sea Lions appears to be robust for now. But the population of Steller Sea Lions is declining in the North Pacific Ocean, and the cause is not fully understood.

# Porpoises, Dolphins and Whales

Porpoises, dolphins and whales belong to the taxonomic order Cetacea, from the Latin word for "whale". Collectively known as cetaceans, these marine mammals are entirely aquatic. Unlike any other group of mammals, they have almost no hair but insulate themselves with a layer of blubber, they have no hind limbs and they breathe through a blowhole on top of the head.

## Harbour Porpoise

Harbour Porpoises are the smallest cetaceans living in the waters of southern Vancouver Island. People rarely see these small, shy animals, though they spend all year here.

A Harbour Porpoise is light grey to brown on the dorsal (back) surface, with lighter sides and usually a white underside. They have a characteristic

Harbour Porpoise.

triangular dorsal fin that is longer in front than behind, and reaches about 20 cm in height. The blow of Harbour Porpoise is rarely visible, but its short puff is clearly audible on a windless day (this gives them the nickname "puffing pigs" in some places). They produce other sounds, too, some ultrasonic and some that humans can hear.

Adults in this region measure up to two metres in length and weigh between 50 and 65 kg, females being larger than males. Newborns are so small (about 5 kg) that they are almost impossible to see. Harbour Porpoises probably live about 20 years.

This region is important to Harbour Porpoises for reproduction and their density can increase ten-fold in summer. The reproductive season runs from May to September. Early in the season females bear single calves (conceived in the previous year), then mate toward the end of summer.

Harbour Porpoises are usually seen in twos or threes, though groups of more than 200 have been recorded in southern Vancouver Island waters. They surface with a gentle rolling motion and rarely breach or display themselves at the surface. But they will fast-surface, making a low splash when feeding in tide lines. Unlike Dall's Porpoises, they rarely approach moving boats. Harbour Porpoises prefer tidally active water less than 150 metres deep. They can dive for as long as five minutes.

In southern British Columbia, they eat squid and a variety of small schooling fishes, including herring, hake and sand lances. In turn, they are hunted by Transient Killer Whales and sharks, though the latter is likely not a significant source of mortality near Victoria. Other threats to their survival are chemical and plastic pollution, entanglement in fishing gear, and habitat degradation by coastal activities.

People report more beach strandings of this species than any other marine mammal in the region. Causes of death range from being struck by a boat to ingestion of plastic to old age. Harbour Porpoises are one of British Columbia's least understood cetaceans with regard to their sociality, population dynamics, natural history and threats. Still, the Committee on the Status of Endangered Wildlife in Canada (COSEWIC) has listed them as

"Special Concern", recognizing that BC's Harbour Porpoises have a "high sensitivity to human activities, are prone to becoming trapped or killed in fishing nets, and are being seen more rarely in highly developed areas such as near Victoria and Haro Strait".

Watch for these shy porpoises on any calm day. Southern Saturna Island and the coast trail of East Sooke Park and Otter Point are good places to catch a glimpse of them from shore. You might also see them while on a ferry between Sidney and Sidney Island, or while travelling to or from Seattle.

## Dall's Porpoise

Dall's Porpoise is probably the most recognized small cetacean in the region, because it will approach a vessel to ride the bow wave. This porpoise can swim as fast as 55 km/h. And it creates a unique "rooster-tail" spray when surfacing quickly, making it easier to find than the Harbour Porpoise. But in recent years the number of Dall's Porpoise sightings has been decreasing in the Victoria area – the reasons for this are not known.

Dall's Porpoise is a stocky cetacean with striking markings. Its body is black with white flank patches, and white on the tip of the dorsal fin, on the trailing edge of the tail flukes and the underside. The upper markings can be seen clearly on mature animals, but are usually less pronounced on younger individuals. Like the Harbour Porpoise, it usually does not have a visible blow.

Dall's Porpoises in southern British Columbia can reach 2.7 metres in length and weigh up to about 220 kg, with males larger than females. The pectoral flippers, tail flukes and head are small in proportion to its robust

Dall's Porpoise.

body. Adult males and females look the same, except during the mating season, when the males develop a pronounced thoracic hump, and a large, well-defined muscle mass on the tailstock. As with Harbour Porpoises, the tiny newborns are difficult to observe in the wild. Dall's Porpoises can live up to 35 years.

The exact timing of this species' mating season in southern BC has not yet been studied. Females give birth to a single calf in the late spring or early summer. Mating follows, from midsummer to early fall. Males physically compete with each other for females.

Dall's Porpoises most often travel in groups of three to five, but occasionally more than a hundred have been seen together. Dive times range from several seconds to about five minutes, and long dives are followed by a series of breaths at the surface only seconds apart. They prefer tidally-active waters more than 150 metres deep. Because of the large muscles on the back and tail of a Dall's Porpoise, its surfacing movement does not look as smooth as that of a Harbour Porpoise.

Most of a Dall's Porpoise's vocalizations are ultrasonic, inaudible to humans. They eat a variety of small fishes and squid, and are eaten by Transient Killer Whales and sharks, although shark predation is likely not significant in this region.

As with the Harbour Porpoise, we know little about the ecology, sociality and effects of human activities on this species, but they are subject to the same dangers posed by pollution and fishing gear.

Your best place to see Dall's Porpoises is from the deck of a boat at sea, but you might occasionally see them from the southern shores of North and South Pender and Saturna islands. Watch for them while on any ferry to or from the Victoria area. The Sidney-Anacortes and the Victoria-Seattle ferries usually pass through good Dall's Porpoise habitats.

## Pacific White-sided Dolphin

Pacific White-sided Dolphins rarely visit the waters around Victoria, but they have been seen. This acrobatic dolphin is known to leap clear of the water and ride in the bow wave of a boat. Most sightings in southern Vancouver Island waters tend to be of large groups, up to about 50 animals, although people occasionally see lone dolphins. The largest groups seen near Victoria have been estimated at about 100; in other areas, groups of Pacific White-sided Dolphins can number more than 1000.

These dolphins are dark bluish-grey with clearly defined light patches on the flanks and a light stripe that runs from the snout to a patch on the tailstock. The dorsal fin is strongly hooked, with a darker front and grey-to-white trailing area. Its blow is rarely visible.

Pacific White-sided Dolphins can reach 2.4 metres in length and weigh up to 150 kg, with males usually larger than females. Newborns are about 1.2 metres long and weigh about 15 kg. The life span is unknown, but could be about 30 years.

Pacific White-sided Dolphins.

These highly social animals produce a variety of squeaks, whistles and clicks – all within the hearing range of humans – for communication, navigation and hunting. Each dolphin produces its own signature whistle.

Pacific White-sided Dolphins have a diet similar to the porpoises in this area; they fall prey to similar predators and suffer the same threats posed by pollution and fishing nets.

There is no good place to watch for Pacific White-sided Dolphins in the Victoria area, because they are so rare here. But you might catch sight of one from a ferry or a boat ride – it's a wonderful species to find.

## Killer Whale

The Killer Whale, or Orca, is the most well-known cetacean in the Victoria region. Members of three different communities of Killer Whales use this area: Resident, Transient and (rarely) Offshore.

Killer Whales can easily be identified by their black-and-white markings. They are black on the dorsal and lateral surfaces, except for a grey-to-white saddle patch behind the dorsal fin, a white eye patch and white patches on the flanks; the underside is mostly white. Males are significantly larger than females, reaching nearly 10 metres long and 5000 kg; females range from 6 to 7 metres in length and weigh up to 4000 kg. Newborn Killer Whales are about 2.5 metres long and weigh about 180 kg. For Resident Killer Whales, it appears that males live 30 to 50 years and females more than 90 years. The life spans of Transient and Offshore Killer Whales have not yet been established.

Killer Whale blows, visible in cool air, have a low, bushy shape. Unlike many other cetaceans, mature male and female Killer Whales can be easily distinguished at the surface. Males have triangular shaped dorsal fins, about two metres tall. Females have hooked dorsal fins that reach a maximum

A female with her calf.

height of only a metre. Juvenile Killer Whales of both sexes have small curved fins.

Both Resident and Transient Killer Whales can be seen near Victoria, especially during the spring, summer and fall. Three Resident pods, known as J, K and L, live here. Their total population fluctuates between about 80 and 100 animals. Residents often swim in groups of about 10, but sometimes during summer and fall, the pods get together to socialize and mate as a superpod. During this time, they become very active at the surface – they breach (jump clear of the water), spy-hop (rise vertically out of the water to about the pectoral fin region), tail lob and tail slap. They also make a lot of noise, and their calls can be heard at the surface without the aid of a hydrophone.

Transient Killer Whales tend to be less surface-active, and sightings of a single animal are not uncommon. Groups of less than five often swim through Victoria waters. More than two hundred Transient Killer Whales have been identified by their individual markings in British Columbian waters.

Spy-hopping.

Females Killer Whales give birth to single calves at any time of year, which indicates less seasonality in the reproductive biology of Killer Whales than many other cetaceans. Calves depend on their mothers for several years. The calving interval is at least two years. Individuals appear to become reproductively active at 15 to 20 years of age.

Resident Killer Whales remain with their maternal families their entire lives, whereas Transients have

Male Resident Killer Whale.

a more dynamic social structure. The life history of Offshore Killer Whales has not yet been studied. All Killer Whales locate family members by sight and sound, and they often use specific contact calls to maintain group cohesiveness at night and when individuals are outside visual range.

In southern Vancouver Island waters, the Resident Killer Whales' preferred prey is salmon, with Chinook Salmon appearing to be their favourite. During the fall, they also target Chum Salmon. But their diet is likely not this simple, and studies currently underway at the Pacific Biological Station should reveal a more complete list of Resident prey species. The local Transient Killer Whales prefer to eat Harbour Seals, California Sea Lions, Steller Sea Lions, Harbour Porpoises and Dall's Porpoises. They sometimes also prey on seabirds. Offshore Killer Whales feed on a variety of fish species, but are thought to specialize on sharks that swim in the deeper waters off Vancouver Island.

COSEWIC has listed the Resident Killer Whales that live in the Victoria area as "Endangered" and Transients as "Threatened". Killer Whales have no natural enemies, but chemical and plastic pollution, declining salmon stocks (for Residents) and human-generated underwater noise are all potential threats to their survival.

Both Resident and Transient Killer Whales pass the shores of the Victoria region throughout the year. Some good places to see them from land are Beechey Head in East Sooke Park, Clover Point in Victoria and occasionally the shores around Saanich Inlet. Any ferry crossing from Victoria, Sidney or Swartz Bay will pass through good Killer Whale habitat.

# Minke Whale

Minke Whales are the smallest baleen whales that regularly visit the waters around Victoria. A baleen whale eats by gulping water or sediment filled with fishes, plankton, crustaceans or other small animals and then trapping the animals in the bristly baleen plates in its mouth as it squeezes out the water.

Minke Whales have a grey-brown back, lighter sides and a white-grey underside. Some have a white stripe across each pectoral flipper, a white chevron pattern across the back just behind the head, or both markings. This sleek whale has a tapered head with a characteristic central ridge. Its small, hooked dorsal fin is approximately two-thirds of the way from the snout to the tail. Fifty to seventy grooves on the skin of the lower jaw allow for expansion of the throat while feeding. This whale has yellow-tan baleen and its blow is low and diffuse.

Minke Whales can reach about eight metres in length and weigh about 10 tons. It is difficult to determine male from female, although females are generally larger. Newborns are about three metres in length and weigh about 350 kg. These whales live for 50 to 60 years.

Biologists have not yet studied the migration patterns and reproductive biology of Minke Whales in British Columbia. In some other regions, these whales migrate to warmer waters during the winter months to mate and bear young. They mate between November and March, and females give birth to a single calf the following winter after a 10- to 11-month gestation period. Minke Whales mature between the ages of five to eight, depending on geographic location.

Most of the time, these whales swim at the leisurely pace of about a couple of kilometres an hour; but when they have to, they can reach speeds up to 44 km/h. Minkes can remain submerged for almost a half an hour, but dives of less than 10 minutes are more common. They communicate by producing a variety of low frequency sounds.

Minke Whales eat small schooling fishes, such as herring and capelins, and large zooplankton, including krill and copepods. Transient Killer Whales and sharks prey on Minke Whales, though the significance of sharks in British Columbia is unknown. Other threats are posed by chemical and plastic pollution, and by ships striking them. In other regions, including some parts of the North Pacific, commercial whalers hunt for this whale.

Late summer and early fall are the best times of year to see Minke Whales around Victoria. People usually see them alone or in groups of up to five individuals. Minkes sometimes breach, but more often they are seen lunge-feeding through a school of small fish. They rarely display any other behaviours on the surface; they do not raise their tail flukes out of the water when beginning a deep dive, as some species do (see Humpback Whale). Minke Whales often give off a sulphur-like smell, which gave rise to their local nickname, the "Stinky Minke".

A feeding Minke Whale draws the attention of gulls looking for scraps.

Minke Whales cannot usually be seen from shore. But a few places have been noted for occasional sightings, including the Victoria breakwater, off Island View Beach and in Ganges Harbour. The Ganges Harbour sighting was probably one of the most spectacular: in 2002, dozens of onlookers witnessed a family of Transient Killer Whales chase a Minke Whale into the harbour, where they killed and ate it.

From a boat, the best places to see Minke Whales are in Haro and Juan de Fuca straits over underwater banks or in areas with upwellings. Watch for them while on a ferry between Victoria and either Seattle or Port Angeles.

## Grey Whale

Grey Whales occasionally swim through Victoria waters during their spring or fall migrations, but not every year. When they appear near Victoria, they tend to remain in the area for at least a few days and sometimes for weeks or months.

These large baleen whales are mottled grey and white, with numerous orange barnacles, yellow whale lice and white-grey scars. Individuals can be identified by the unique patterns on their backs and tails. They do not have a dorsal fin, but instead a low hump about two-thirds of the way along the back and a series of 6 to 12 smaller bumps descending along the tailstock. The head has many small depressions that contain whiskers, and the throat has two to five deep creases. The broad tail flukes lift out of the water before the whale makes a deep dive. The baleen is a pale yellow and the spout takes the shape of an elongated heart.

Adult Grey Whales can reach 14 metres in length and weigh 35 tons. Males and females look the same, although females are generally larger.

The invertebrate-encrusted back of a Grey Whale.

Newborns are 5 metres long and weigh up to 500 kg. The lifespan of a Grey Whale ranges from 50 to 80 years.

Grey Whales undertake one of the longest migrations of any mammal. They spend summer in the cold waters of the Bering Sea and winter in the warm waters around Baja California – a 20,000-km round trip. Most Grey Whales swim all the way to the Bering Sea in spring, but approximately 200 remain in British Columbia and Washington for the summer. These are known as resident Grey Whales.

Calves are born and mating occurs in the warm Mexican waters of Baja from January to March. Females bear young every second year from maturity (which begins at 5 to 11 years of age) following a 13-month gestation period. Most calves are born in January and rapidly increase in size (about 90 kg/day) before beginning the northward migration. Grey Whales are very active and social with their calves. Lactation lasts six to nine months.

Grey Whales, especially mothers with calves, stay closer to shore than most other large whale species. They travel up to 10 km/h and can cover about 130 km per day on a migration, with swim speeds increasing as they get closer to their destination.

These baleen whales feed primarily during the summer months while in cold temperate and subarctic waters. They eat bottom-dwelling invertebrates, such as molluscs, gastropods and crustaceans, but also plankton, such as crab larvae and herring roe. They rarely prey on fishes, but they have been observed eating anchovies. When feeding at the ocean bottom, they often return to the surface with their heads covered in muddy sediment, and their feeding can be tracked by the underwater muddy plumes that they create. Because most Grey Whales turn on their right side to scoop up the fine muddy sediments, they often have fewer barnacles on the right side of the face and jaw.

While migrating, Grey Whales dive for less than 5 minutes, but in the north they can remain submerged for up to 20 minutes when feeding. They have been reported to dive to 120 metres below the surface, though they usually keep to shallower waters for feeding.

Grey Whales make a variety of low-frequency calls during the day and night, audible to people as moans, clicks, squeaks and roars. One of the most surface-active species of large whales, they are often seen spy-hopping, lob-tailing and breaching, usually in the southern breeding grounds, but sometimes in British Columbia's waters.

Because of their regular migration and tendency to stay close to the coast, Grey Whales were easy targets for whalers, who hunted them nearly to extinction by the early 1900s. Since then, conservation measures have helped the recovery of the population in the northeastern Pacific, which is now at about 17,000. It is the only population of Grey Whales to recover from the effects of commercial whaling. These whales are still hunted in the far north, and sporadic whaling openings have occurred in Washington. Widespread threats to this species include entanglement in fishing gear, underwater noise, pollution and collisions with ships.

Around Victoria, good places to view Grey Whales during the spring and fall migrations include Sooke, Oak Bay, Cordova Bay and Sidney. Only occasionally are Grey Whales sighted in the Gulf Islands.

## Humpback Whale

Humpback Whales visit the coastal waters of British Columbia as part of their summer feeding range. Long ago, commercial whaling decimated the local population. But they now appear regularly in the waters off Victoria. Sightings are much more common than they were just a decade ago.

Humpback Whales are dark blue-grey to black, with white on the pectoral fins and underside of the tail flukes. They have a number of large hair-follicle knobs and often barnacles on the snout. The snout and body may be scarred, mostly caused during mating competitions. The pectoral fins are

A breaching Humpback Whale.

The knobby snout of a Humpback.

exceptionally long, up to a third of the entire body length. A small dorsal fin rises from the back about two-thirds the way from the nose to the tail flukes. These whales have 12 to 36 throat grooves, and the baleen is dark olive to black. Their blow is a tall column that extends two to three metres above the sea surface.

The pigmentation pattern on the tail flukes is unique to each animal and enables researchers to identify individuals. Before a deep dive, a Humpback Whale strongly arches its tailstock in a distinctive hump, and usually raises its tail flukes out of the water.

Humpback Whales are the largest cetaceans to pay regular visits to Victoria's waters. They can reach 16 metres in length and weigh up to 40 tons; females are generally larger than males. As with most whales, it is difficult to determine the sex of an individual, except when a female swims with her calf. Newborn calves are 4 to 5 metres long and weigh up to 2 tons. These whales can live for 80 years.

Humpback Whales migrate between the warm waters of Mexico and Hawaii and the cold waters of British Columbia and Alaska. They are mostly reproductively active during the winter and spring months in southern waters. Females bear single calves in winter after nearly a year of gestation. Calves take about six months to wean to an adult diet.

Adults feed mostly on small fishes, such as herring, sand lances, sardines and smelt; they also eat krill. Humpbacks have developed an interesting technique, called bubble-netting, to capture prey. A whale takes in air before a dive and then releases it while swimming in a circle below the surface. The air bubbles rise in a circular column up to 45 metres in diameter, trapping the fishes inside long enough for the whale to gulp them up.

Humpback Whales swim slowly and can remain submerged for up to 45 minutes. These long dives are more common in the breeding grounds, which is where the males "sing" as part of their mating behaviour. Transient Killer Whales and sharks will prey on young Humpbacks during a migration, but adults have no natural predators.

This species tends to return to the same places year after year, so human activities in or adjacent to these habitats can affect the whales that

Humpback raising its tail flukes as it dives.

visit them. Collisions with ships, pollution and habitat degradation threaten Humpback Whales. COSEWIC has listed this species as "Special Concern".

It's difficult to see Humpback Whales from shore in the Victoria area. But sightings in Juan de Fuca Strait have been increasing in frequency over the past decade. The best chance of observing a Humpback Whale is from a ferry between Victoria and either Port Angeles or Seattle, especially from August to October. Late summer and early autumn whale-watching trips can offer good chances of seeing Humpback Whales.

## Uncommon Visitors

While on a boat travelling in Victoria waters you might be lucky enough to see one or a group of these infrequent visitors: Fin Whales, False Killer Whales, Risso's Dolphins, Northern Right Whale Dolphins or a species of beaked whale. But your chances are low on the water and almost non-existent from shore.

## Conservation

Marine mammals are vulnerable to chemical and noise pollution, the hazards associated with fishing, global climate change and habitat loss. Our efforts to reduce ocean litter and pesticide runoff into storm drains and beach areas will help protect all marine life. As coastal residents, we need to ensure that the marine mammals of British Columbia are treated with respect.

# Marine Mammal Viewing Guidelines*

When you have an opportunity to watch a marine mammal while on the water, please follow these guidelines:

- Always approach areas of known or suspected marine wildlife activity slowly, and reduce speed to less than seven knots when within 400 metres of the nearest whale.
- If whales approach you, move cautiously out of the way.
- Stay on the offshore side of whales when they are travelling close to shore.
- Always approach and move away from whales from the side, roughly parallel to the direction the whales are heading.
- Do not approach or position your boat closer than 100 metres to any whale.
- If your boat drifts within 100 metres, place the engine in neutral and allow whales to pass.
- Do not drive through groups of porpoises or dolphins to encourage bow or stern-riding.
- If dolphins or porpoises choose to ride the bow wave of your boat, avoid sudden course changes; hold your course and speed or reduce your speed gradually.
- Be cautious and quiet when around seal or sea-lion haul-outs and seabird colonies, especially during breeding, nesting and pupping seasons (generally May to September).
- Always reduce speed to minimize the wake, wash and noise of your boat, and then slowly pass without stopping, paying attention to signs of disturbance or agitation.
- Do not disturb, swim with, move, feed or touch any marine mammal, including seal pups.
- Report injured, distressed or dead marine mammals to the Department of Fisheries and Oceans Canada hotline at 1-800-465-4336.

There are many good whale-watching operators on southern Vancouver Island. When choosing one, ask about whether or not the operator adheres to wildlife viewing guidelines, and about species seasonality, viewing conditions and the experience of the crew.

---

* Modified by the editors from the Cetus Society's "Marine Wildlife Guidelines for Boaters, Paddlers and Viewers" (http://cetussociety.org/education/whale-watching-guidelines).

# Nearshore Fishes

## Gavin Hanke

The intertidal zone of the Victoria region supports many fish species, and these fishes are part of food webs that link the land and sea. Many birds, terrestrial mammals and even garter snakes will venture into the intertidal zone to eat fishes exposed at low tide. Even our harbours and docks, with all their industrial and recreational activity, support communities of fishes, from the superabundant Surfperch and Three-spined Stickleback, to the Bay Pipefish, a relative of the sea horse that looks more like a strand of seaweed than a fish. Some of our nearshore fishes are particularly attractive and outlandish in shape, and have fascinating adaptations to life in the shallows.

Some may ask why we should bother studying intertidal fishes – most of them are not economically important – but they do serve as food for game fishes and other wildlife in British Columbia. For example, the Pacific Sandlance is one of the most important food-fishes along the coast and their populations support a wide range of predators. These silvery, slender fishes may be seen burrowing or emerging from sand or gravel beaches, or travelling in schools in shallows or offshore. Sandlances and other non-game fishes are part of the complex ecosystems of our marine coastline, and aside from their potential to support fisheries that humans exploit, they are part of the global ecosystem which is irreplaceable. For that reason non-game fishes are worthy of study and protection.

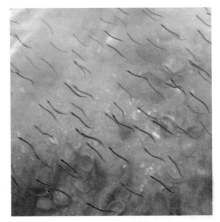

Pacific Sandlances schooling in shallow water.

We can expect significant change in intertidal and nearshore habitat along our coastline within 100 years through the effects of climate change. Shallow water environments, marine algae and invertebrates exposed as tide falls, and tide pools and their contents may endure greater extremes in summer versus winter temperatures, radical temperature changes within each tidal cycle, and also increased rainfall in some seasons or no rain for long periods of time. It is likely that nearshore organisms will show a response to climate warming much earlier than deep-water species.

Other threats to our local coastline ecosystems are more immediate. These include pollution such as spilled fuels, run-off from roads, chemicals from outfalls and plastic litter on our shorelines. The threat from oil or spilled fuel is obvious and large spills are news-worthy, but the other litter is not only unsightly, it may be accidentally ingested by marine life and may trap or ensnare animals. The effects of litter on marine mammals and birds has been well documented, but its effects on intertidal fishes are largely unknown. Not surprisingly, you will find that tide pool and nearshore ecological diversity increases as you explore farther away from large coastal cities and busy harbours.

It is not easy to identify all species of intertidal fishes without a microscope and a preserved specimen, and young fish are especially difficult. But many of the general groupings of fishes are relatively easy to identify. Any of the rocky shorelines in our area boast a decent population of intertidal fishes, even areas fairly close to Victoria's and Esquimalt's harbours. East Sooke Park is a great place to explore, and within a short walk, you can find sandy beaches and rocky shores that provide hours of entertainment.

In this chapter I describe some of the more common species that people will encounter. For more information on identifying nearshore and tide pool fishes I recommend *Coastal Fishes of the Pacific Northwest*, a field guide packed with colour photographs and useful information to help any curious naturalist (see Lamb and Edgell in Additional Reading, page 214).

Tidal pools appear at low tide, like here at Clover Point.

A Tidepool Sculpin caught in a shallow tidal pool.

## High in the Intertidal Zone

High in the intertidal zone you are likely to see only the Tidepool Sculpin, probably the most common intertidal fish in British Columbia. These hardy fishes vary in colour and pattern, are tolerant of the rapidly changing conditions characteristic of tide pools nearer the high tide line. They also range throughout the intertidal zone. High in the intertidal zone, fishes have to endure rapid changes in temperature as the sun heats the water in tide pools and rainfall dilutes it –trapped fishes can experience cold, salty water changing to warm, almost fresh water within hours.

Smaller tide pools may have one or two Tidepool Sculpins, but larger pools can support hundreds. Tidepool Sculpins are mottled grey and red-brown to green, with prominent bands running obliquely down the body. These sculpins also get stranded on beaches under woody debris, rocks and marine algae as the tide recedes; as long as their gills stay moist and cool, these hardy fishes can survive out of water for several hours. They can also be seen within centimetres of shore as the flood tide reclaims beach real estate – these fishes live on the edge. Tidepool Sculpins are often the only intertidal fishes seen by beachcombers because of their abundance and presence near the high-tide mark.

## Midway in the Intertidal Zone

Lower in the intertidal zone, tide pools support more diverse algae and invertebrate communities, and these in turn support more species of fishes than can be found near the high tide mark. Pools midway in the intertidal zone are not exposed for as long a period when the tide is out, and so the conditions in each pool are more stable, remaining closer to that of normal sea water. Such pools may have dense carpets of anemones, more diverse communities of gastropods and crabs, and a few more marine algae species, including coralline algae, which appear like branching strings of pink-white beads, or as pink mats encrusting any solid surface. The diversity and colour in these tide pools rewards the naturalist curious enough to venture below the high-tide mark.

Fishes midway down the intertidal zone are not as tolerant of extremes in environmental change as the Tidepool Sculpin. Crescent Gunnels, High Cockscombs, Tidepool Sculpins and the occasional Northern Clingfish are a few species that can regularly be found here. Most of these fishes either reside under shelter, or take shelter as people approach a tide pool. You will also find these fishes in pockets beneath rocks on a beach where it stays cool and moist, even where it appears that there is no standing water.

People often find long, wriggling fishes under intertidal rocks and they proclaim that they have found eels. These are not eels, but gunnels or pricklebacks, with spiny dorsal fins similar to those of surfperch, rockfish or bass. Their closest relatives among our marine fishes are eelpouts – also not closely related to eels.

Many intertidal fishes cannot be observed unless you move a rock or two. Clingfish use their modified pelvic fins to stick to the underside of rocks, while gunnels, pricklebacks and sculpins hide under rocks until the tide returns. It is impossible to move any rocks in the intertidal zone without impacting some form of life, so it is our responsibility to do as little

Fishes often found under rocks midway or low in the intertidal zone (top to bottom): Crescent Gunnel, High Cockscomb, Rock Prickleback and Northern Clingfish.

damage as possible while exploring these fascinating environments. Even when walking along rocks, we unwittingly crush barnacles, mussels, and tiny snails with each footfall. Be extremely careful when lifting rocks, and be sure to replace rocks gently, exactly where you found them to avoid unnecessary loss of life and habitat.

## Low in the Intertidal Zone

The lowermost pools along any stretch of shoreline are among the most amazing and fascinating environments to explore. Not only do these pools have regular inhabitants, but they occasionally trap fishes that live in deeper water. A four-metre-long Pacific Sleeper Shark once got stranded in a tide pool in Alaska – so you never know what you might find.

The lowermost tide pools usually contain a diverse community of crabs, gastropods, nudibranchs, anemones, urchins, sea stars, calcareous algae and sponges. Marine macroalgae commonly forms a rich aquatic forest that drapes over rocks as the tide recedes. The algae laying over the rocks makes exploration a bit more slippery and tricky compared to higher in the intertidal zone, but well worth the effort. The layer of macroalgae also forms a great shield from the heat of the sun and many fishes can be found sheltered underneath, even in the smallest pools near the low-tide line.

The lowermost pools are accessible only when the tide is fully out (see page 101 for details about local tides). As a result, you may need to go exploring at odd hours to be sure you hit low tide, and you will only have a short time at slack low tide to explore pools for marine life – so pick your pools carefully. It is best to scout out areas in advance for prospective rock pools. One of the more forgiving spots to view pools right at low tide is Clover Point. The area is level and fairly safe, with loads of pools to explore. In contrast, some pools around Cattle Point's boat launch in Oak Bay can be foul and not as pleasant in summer (except for filamentous algae enthusiasts).

Blades of marine algae shelter tiny pools and niches around rocks in the lowest part of the intertidal zone.

Some common fishes that you can see on a regular basis in tide pools in the Victoria region include: Crescent Gunnels, Penpoint Gunnels, High Cockscombs, Rock Pricklebacks, Black Pricklebacks, Tidepool Sculpins, Padded

Fishes found in the low intertidal zone (clockwise from top left): Padded Sculpin, Blackeye Goby, Kelp Poacher, White-spotted Greenling, Rockhead and Tidepool Snailfish.

Sculpins, Buffalo Sculpins, Northern Clingfish, Tidepool Snailfish and the occasional White-spotted Greenling. This list is far from complete, so you can expect to make many discoveries, such as the bizarre Rockhead and Kelp Poacher, and a range of other small sculpins. If you are really lucky, you may find a Grunt Sculpin, a Pacific Spiny Lumpsucker or a Blackeye Goby, although these usually are subtidal and rarely trapped in tide pools.

I have caught a few Longfin Sculpins in breeding colours below the tideline on the east side of Clover Point. These gorgeous fishes are fast, and in breeding dress have alternating fine bands of bright red and blue.

## Sandy Beaches

Sandy beaches constantly change with waves and tides, so life on the beach has to avoid being buried by shifting sands or left high and dry at the mercy of the sun and scavengers, or children with pointed sticks. The fishes living in shallows along sandy beaches tend to be sparsely distributed, so you will have to wade for a while to appreciate the beach's diversity. Some beaches

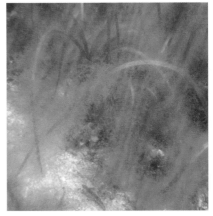

The Staghorn Sculpin (top) and Butter Sole (bottom right) are common along sandy beaches, but Pacific Spiny Lumpsuckers (bottom left) and many other nearshore fishes concentrate near eel-grass beds.

have Common Eel-grass beds, and these present a structural oasis for fishes. You can expect far more fishes to reside in and around the shelter of eel-grass beds, and for the same reason, any isolated rock may act as cover and house a fish or two. Once, while exploring Willows Beach in Oak Bay, I lifted a rock on an otherwise barren sandy area and found a single seven-centimetre-long Roselip Sculpin underneath. At Witty's Lagoon, you can find young flatfish and Staghorn Sculpins, and even larger Starry Flounder in knee-deep water. Where there is any structure, you may be pleasantly surprised at what you find.

If you have access to a beach seine net, one sweep through an eel-grass bed will yield an even greater variety of fishes, most of which would be virtually invisible if you just waded through the area. An evening beach seine in December 2011 resulted in a school of Tubesnouts, a few Bay Pipefish, a White-spotted Greenling, a Striped Seaperch, a few Walleye Pollock, a Starry Flounder and an array of sculpins. The first seine in open water came up almost empty, but the second passed through the eel-grass bed and was full of fishes. Fish love structure in their lives.

A young greenling (lower centre) in an eel-grass bed in the sandy flats at Willow's Beach.

# Mud Flats and Estuaries

Mud flats and estuaries offer an experience beyond all others. One step in the wrong direction and you can find yourself slipping from hard packed sand in a stream channel into knee deep smelly mud in an eel-grass bed. These muddy habitats are rich with life and so it is well worth spending some time slopping around in search of fishes. Eel-grass beds can be thick in estuaries and muddy bays and these are great places to search for near-shore fishes. The upper end of Victoria's inner harbour is nice and muddy and it is fun to float along in a canoe or kayak to watch fishes in the shallows. As the tide recedes, fishes retreat to any cover that remains moist and sheltered from the sun. The area around the mouth of the Sooke River or Metchosin Creek (Witty's Lagoon) also presents hours of fun to those interested in exploring sloppy seashores.

Estuaries (where freshwater streams meet the sea) harbour a restricted group of fishes, and the flowing water of creeks and rivers provides a bit more firm footing for fish-friendly naturalists. Estuaries also provide a curious mix of freshwater and marine fishes, and at times, also harbour young smelt and salmon.

If you drift along in the shallows you can expect to see schools of Surfperch, Pacific Herring, Three-spined Stickleback and Bay Pipefish swimming around. On the bottom, a range of flatfish, Staghorn Sculpins, Crescent Gunnels and Sturgeon Poachers may be seen. Bay and Arrow gobies share burrows with shrimp, and if you are really lucky, you will get a good look at these tiny fishes before they dart for safety. Even the Prickly Sculpin, a denizen of freshwater, can be found in the lower reaches of estuaries.

# Docksides

Docks, piers, rock walls and other artificial structures in our harbours provide cover for a great variety of marine organisms. A walk along a pier will reveal many species of marine algae, sponges, barnacles, mussels, sea stars, polychaete worms, anemones and much more. These encrusting organisms also do a great job of coating stationary objects and providing ample cover for coastal fishes.

Observation of dockside fishes is a little difficult because the wary animals will retreat to deeper water or under the dock itself. In the open water around a dock, you can expect to see Tubesnouts, Pacific Herring, Surfperches, White-spotted Greenlings, Bay Pipefish and Three-spined Sticklebacks. Tubesnouts are particularly attractive when in their June breeding dress – they have a dark body, a bright orange spot on each pectoral fin, bright red pelvic fins and a bright blue snout. Crescent Gunnels are common, as well as small sculpins that forage among the invertebrates encrusting dock pilings. You might also see young rockfish cruising in search of

Some of the common fishes around docks in our region (top to bottom): Three-spined Stickleback (left) and Starry Flounder; Silver-spotted Sculpin (left) and Copper Rockfish; Bay Pipefish; Tubesnout.

prey, but not usually near the surface. In some places, young salmon can be superabundant at certain times as they pass docks on their way out into the ocean. Flatfishes and sculpins are common on the bottom underneath and around docks, but they are visible only in shallows nearer shore, by angling, or to the aquanaut who dares to venture between dock piles.

## How to Catch and View Fishes Safely

When we look at fishes in tide pools, in shallows along shore and alongside docks, we view them from above. But fishes really come to life when viewed from the side, as we would see them in an aquarium. It would be awkward to carry a glass or acrylic viewing tank every time you go for a beach walk. Instead, a clear plastic bag makes a light-weight temporary aquarium to hold small fishes for a short while. Put plenty of water in the bag. Fishes can then be enjoyed for a few minutes and released unharmed.

A transluscent young flatfish shows a rainbow effect from light refraction while being held temporarily in a bag for observation.

Some of our coastal fishes are fairly slow and can be caught by hand – try herding sculpins to the shallow edge of a tide pool and then cup the fish in your hand. Prickle-backs and gunnels are really tough to catch by hand – as they wriggle wildly and are extremely slippery – so use a dip net to catch them. A Snailfish or Northern Clingfish can be coaxed off kelp or rocks by gently moving it side-to-side or forward and backward to convince it to let go; don't pull it straight away from the rock, because you may harm the fish; be patient and wait until it lets go. The Grunt Sculpin, Kelp Poacher, Pacific Spiny Lumpsucker and Rock-head are the slowest tide pool fishes and can be caught by hand without any real chase.

To catch faster fishes, any simple dip net from a pet shop will work. I tend to use one hand to herd fishes toward a waiting dip net rather than flailing around with the dip net itself. This technique is easy on the tide pool and its inhabitants and also minimizes the risk of the dip net snagging on rocks and barnacles. A net with a 10-15 cm opening is the best size. Larger nets get cumbersome in small spaces, and fish can easily avoid smaller nets. Green or black nets are better than white nets because they blend with the background and may not be so obvious to fishes. Try to avoid catching too much gravel and debris in the net because a struggling fish can do damage to itself on shell fragments and gravel.

Submersible digital cameras provide a high-tech solution to fish viewing. You may be able to buy a simple underwater housing for your own pocket digital camera. For tide pool photography, where depth and lighting are of no concern, any underwater case or camera will work, but if you'd like to do underwater photography while snorkelling or diving, it would be better to do a bit more research into underwater photography and invest in some decent equipment.

## Conservation

Other than the indirect benefits to marine mammals, coastal birds and coastal fisheries, it may be hard to justify to the average person why tiny intertidal fishes (and for that matter, the rest of the intertidal community) are worth any concern compared to other high-profile ecosystems in this province. Intertidal communities form a link between terrestrial and marine ecosystems, so understanding them is crucial to making informed decisions regarding habitat preservation and management of human activities.

Quillback Rockfish sometimes get caught in crab traps.

Only recently has there been a greater appreciation for the link between Pacific salmon and coastal forest ecosystems. The recognition that changes in marine ecosystems can profoundly affect something as radically different as a coastal rainforest should remind us that all of this planet's ecosystems are connected and influence each other. Everything we do to our shorelines has trickle-down effects elsewhere, however subtle, and so the study of intertidal communities and their connectedness has value – even if only to minimize our impacts on neighbouring economically exploited ecosystems.

Our homes and industries are concentrated around harbours and estuaries. Beaches are used by people for recreation, and the majority of people would prefer a natural, unpolluted shore. But it would be difficult to find a stretch of British Columbia's coast without some form of garbage or chemical contamination. Pollution levels will not likely drop in the near future, especially with the growing human population, so it is important to take the time now to learn as much as we can about our natural world, before we lose more biodiversity. In their book, *Basking Sharks: the Slaughter of BC's Gentle Giants* (see Additional Reading, page 214), Scott Wallace and Brian Gisborne discuss the concept of "shifting baseline syndrome" – what was normal to our grandparents seems completely foreign to the next generation, and even more so to successive generations, because each generation gets used to the prevailing conditions and the incremental lowering of standards with respect to nature. One has to wonder what our world will be like in the next 200 years given the pace of change in the last two centuries.

Fortunately, despite years of abuse, our coastal ecosystems have proven fairly resistant to change and you can still find areas with rich nearshore fish communities. Low tides in June can be great for fish-watching, especially since many of our most interesting tide pool fishes are found in the lowest parts of the intertidal zone. Intertidal life is readily accessible to everyone who cares to look, and a careful walk on the beach is a great way to introduce children to the wonders of nature. It also is more important than ever that adults spend the time to explore beaches and our tidal waters, even if for nothing more than to gain an appreciation of what we stand to lose if we fail to adequately protect this planet and our environment.

## Scientific Names of Species Mentioned in this Chapter

| | |
|---|---|
| Arrow Goby | *Clevelandia ios* |
| Bay Goby | *Lepidogobius lepidus* |
| Bay Pipefish | *Syngnathus leptorhynchus* |
| Blackeye Goby | *Coryphopterus nicholsi* |
| Black Prickleback | *Xiphister atropurpureus* |
| Buffalo Sculpin | *Enophrys bison* |
| Butter Sole | *Isopsetta isolepis* |
| Coastrange Sculpin | *Cottus aleuticus* |
| Copper Rockfish | *Sebastes caurinus* |
| Crescent Gunnel | *Pholis laeta* |
| Dogfish | *Squalus suckleyi* |
| Grunt Sculpin | *Rhamphocottus richardsoni* |
| High Cockscomb | *Anoplarchus purpurescens* |
| Kelp Poacher | *Agonomalus mozinoi* |
| Longfin Sculpin | *Jordania zonope* |
| Northern Clingfish | *Gobiesox maeandricus* |
| Pacific Herring | *Clupea pallasi* |
| Pacific Sandlance | *Ammodytes hexapterus* |
| Pacific Sleeper Shark | *Somionosus pacificus* |
| Pacific Spiny Lumpsucker | *Eumicrotremus orbis* |
| Padded Sculpin | *Artedius fenestralis* |
| Penpoint Gunnel | *Apodichthys flavidus* |
| Plainfin Midshipman | *Porichthys notatus* |
| Prickly Sculpin | *Cottus asper* |
| Quillback Rockfish | *Sebastes maliger* |
| Ratfish | *Hydrolagus colliei* |
| Rockhead | *Bothragonus swani* |
| Rock Pricklebacks | *Xiphister mucosus* |
| Roselip Sculpin | *Ascelichthys rhodurus* |
| Silver-spotted Sculpin | *Blepsias cirrhosus* |
| Staghorn Sculpin | *Leptocottus armatus* |
| Starry Flounder | *Platichthys stellatus* |
| Sturgeon Poacher | *Agonus acipenserinus* |
| Surfperch | *Cymatogaster aggregatum* |
| Tadpole Sculpins | *Psychrolutes paradoxus* |
| Three-spined Stickleback | *Gasterosteus aculeatus* |
| Tidepool Sculpin | *Oligocottus maculosus* |
| Tidepool Snailfish | *Liparis florae* |
| Tubesnout | *Aulorhnchus flavidus* |
| White-spotted Greenling | *Hexagrammos stelleri* |

# Plants

**Leon E. Pavlick**
**Revised and updated by**
**the Victoria Natural History Society**

Plant life in the Victoria region reflects mild, moist winters, relatively dry summers and diversity in topography and soils. Victoria is in the Georgia Basin, a part of the extreme southwest corner of British Columbia, and has the lowest rainfall in Canada during midsummer. This is the result of a ridge of high pressure that develops off the west coast, and also because of the rainshadow effect of the Olympic Mountains in Washington and the Vancouver Island Mountains.

The east side of southern Vancouver Island, including Victoria, Saanich Peninsula, Colwood, Metchosin and East Sooke, receives less rainfall than the west side. These two areas interface around Goldstream and Metchosin, though the changes in vegetetation become more striking in the Sooke-Jordan River area.

A wildflower meadow.

The bare trunks of Arbutus trees.

Garry Oak meadow with camas in bloom.

In the Victoria region, less moisture is available to plants on the summits of the hills and mountains than in the valleys, due to soil conditions and topography. The amount of moisture available increases as you go downhill. The dry, rocky summits of some of the low mountains and hills around Victoria have open areas on them, termed "grass balds". Immediately downslope there is often a band of Garry Oak woodland and below this, Douglas-fir forest. On moister sites, such as valley bottoms and seepage areas, the forest composition changes. Large Douglas-fir trees may be present on some sites, but Western Redcedar, Sword Fern, Grand Fir and Red Alder are the dominant species of these moister forests. Wet forests take over in depressions and on the margins of streams, lakes and ponds.

For those new to this area, some species merit special mention. The striking tree with smooth, red-brown bark that grows on rocky bluffs and in poor soils is the Arbutus (*Arbutus menziesii*). It is our only broadleaved evergreen tree. The only native oak you will see is the Garry Oak (*Quercus garryana*). Douglas-fir (*Pseudotsuga menziesii*) is the most common upland needle-leaved evergreen. The maple tree with leaves much wider than your hand is the Bigleaf Maple (*Acer macrophyllum*). Indian Plum (*Oemleria cerasiformis*) is the first native shrub to bloom in the spring – February or March – closely followed by the Red-flowering Currant (*Ribes sanguineum*). Much later, another native shrub puts on a spectacular show – watch for drifts of creamy Oceanspray (*Holodiscus discolor*) blossoms in June as you walk along hedgerows throughout the region.

Two species of camas, Common Camas (*Camassia quamash*) and Great Camas (*Camassia leichtlinii*), can still be found in many open areas with patches of relatively deep soil. The bulbs of these species are a traditionally important source of carbohydrates for the First Nations of the region,

White Fawn Lily.

and historically open meadows were actively maintained through the use of controlled burns. Watch for these gorgeous purple beauties in many of our protected areas. Imagine stately Garry Oaks surrounded by a "sea" of camas – that is what much of the area looked like when the first European explorers arrived.

The White Fawn Lily (*Erythronium oregonum*) puts on spectacular displays in the late March and April woodlands. In May the large blooms of the Western Flowering Dogwood (*Cornus nuttallii*) brighten up some Douglas-fir forests. In June watch the woods for a ghostly white plant called Indian Pipe (*Monotropa uniflora*). It doesn't have any of its own green-pigmented chlorophyll to generate energy from sunlight. Instead it gets its energy by parasitizing fungi that have formed a mycorrhizal association with the trees. Because it is not dependent on sunlight, it can grow in very dark environments in the understorey of a dense forest. In the sunnier areas of the forest the evergreen Salal (*Gaultheria shallon*) is a crowd-pleaser in any season.

In wet places in the spring, a dramatic sight and scent is provided by the enormous yellow spathe of Skunk Cabbage (*Lysichiton americanum*), also known as Swamp Lantern. Along hedgerows a white-berried shrub, Common Snowberry (*Symphoricarpos albus*), grows in abundance. It is most apparent in the fall and winter, because the white berries are not preferred by wildlife and often hang on until spring. In contrast, the white berries of Red-osier Dogwood (*Cornus stolonifera*) are considered delicious by many birds and quickly disappear. Instead it is the beautiful red stems of these shrubs that provides winter interest.

Satinflower (above) and Blue-eyed Mary.

# Grass Balds and Garry Oak Woodlands

Grass balds are open areas in which the vegetation is largely grasses and other herbaceous plants. In the Victoria region they characterize rocky, steep southerly slopes that have little soil. The Garry Oak woodland has an abundance of lower vegetation distributed throughout the stand of oaks. Soils may be deep or shallow in balds and woodlands, and the latter often occurs on rock outcrops. The herbaceous floras of the woodlands and grass balds are similar and spectacular. Flower-watching starts early here.

**February to early March:**

| | |
|---|---|
| Blue-eyed Mary | *Collinsia parviflora* and *C. grandiflora* |
| Chickweed Monkey-flower | *Mimulus alsinoides* |
| Spring Gold | *Lomatium utriculatum* |
| Rusty-haired Saxifrage | *Saxifraga rufidula* |
| Satinflower | *Olsynium douglasii* |

**Late March to early April:**

| | |
|---|---|
| Broad-leaved Shootingstar | *Dodecatheon hendersonii* |
| Chickweed Monkey-flower | *Mimulus alsinoides* |
| Common Camas | *Camassia quamash* |
| Miner's-lettuce | *Claytonia perfoliata* |
| Seablush | *Plectritis congesta* |
| Small-leaved Montia | *Montia parvifolia* |
| Tall Oregon-grape | *Mahonia aquifolium* |
| Western Buttercup | *Ranunculus occidentalis* |
| White Fawn Lily | *Erythronium oregonum* |

**Late April to mid May:**

| | |
|---|---|
| Chocolate Lily | *Fritillaria affinis* |
| Cleavers | *Galium aparine* |
| Common Snowberry | *Symphoricarpos albus* |
| Common Vetch | *Vicia sativa* (I) |

| | |
|---|---|
| Dovefoot Geranium | *Geranium molle* (I) |
| Few-flowered Clover | *Trifolium oliganthum* |
| Field Chickweed | *Cerastium arvense* |
| Garry Oak | *Quercus garryana* |
| Great Camas | *Camassia leichtlinii* |
| Hairy Honeysuckle | *Lonicera hispidula* |
| Menzies' Larkspur | *Delphinium menziesii* |
| Meadow Death-camas | *Zigadenus venenosus* |
| Pacific Sanicle | *Sanicula crassicaulis* |
| Purple Peavine | *Lathyrus nevadensis* |
| Scotch Broom | *Cytisus scoparius* (I) |
| Small-flowered Alumroot | *Heuchera micrantha* |
| Small-flowered Bird's-foot Trefoil | *Lotus micranthus* |
| Tomcat Clover | *Trifolium willdenowii* |

### Late May to mid June:

| | |
|---|---|
| Broadleaf Stonecrop | *Sedum spathulifolium* |
| Fool's Onion | *Triteleia hyacinthina* |
| Harvest Brodiaea | *Brodiaea coronaria* |
| Hooker's Onion | *Allium acuminatum* |
| Woolly Eriophyllum | *Eriophyllum lanatum* |
| Yarrow | *Achillea millefolium* |

### Some grasses you may find:

| | |
|---|---|
| Barren Brome | *Bromus sterilis* (I) |
| Blue Wildrye | *Elymus glaucus* |
| Hedgehog Dogtail | *Cynosurus echinatus* (I) |
| California Brome | *Bromus carinatus* |
| California Oatgrass | *Danthonia californica* |
| Cheatgrass | *Bromus tectorum* (I) |
| Rattail Fescue | *Vulpia myuros* (I) |
| Early Hairgrass | *Aira praecox* (I) |
| Roemer's Fescue | *Festuca idahoensis roemeri* |
| Soft Brome | *Bromus hordeaceus* |

Broadleaf Stonecrop.

Clockwise from top left: Harvest Brodiaea, Menzie's Larkspur, Chocolate Lily, Hairy Honeysuckle, Woolly Eriophyllum.

Male and female
Douglas-fir cones.

## Douglas-fir Forests

In respect to moisture requirements, Douglas-fir forest lies between that
of the drier Garry Oak woodland and the wetter Western Redcedar/Sword
Fern forest. Douglas-fir is always present. Drier sites have an Arbutus-
Douglas-fir association, and moister sites have a Douglas-fir-Oregon-grape
association. Watch for the following species.

**February and March:**

| | |
|---|---|
| Indian Plum | *Oemleria cerasiformis* |
| Red Alder | *Alnus rubra* |
| Pacific Sanicle | *Sanicula crassicaulis* |
| Red-flowering Currant | *Ribes sanguineum* |
| White Fawn Lily | *Erythronium oregonum* |

**April:**

| | |
|---|---|
| Arbutus | *Arbutus menziesii* |
| Bigleaf Maple | *Acer macrophyllum* |
| Fairy Slipper | *Calypso bulbosa* |
| Douglas-fir | *Pseudotsuga menziesii* |

| | |
|---|---|
| Small-flowered Nemophila | *Nemophila parviflora* |
| Siberian Miner's Lettuce | *Claytonia sibirica* |
| Western Trillium | *Trillium ovatum* |
| White Fawn Lily | *Erythronium oregonum* |

**May:**

| | |
|---|---|
| Bearded Fescue | *Festuca subulata* |
| Broadleaved Starflower | *Trientalis borealis* |
| Cascara | *Rhamnus purshiana* |
| Columbia Brome | *Bromus vulgaris* |
| Sweet-scented Bedstraw | *Galium triflorum* |
| Grand Fir | *Abies grandis* |
| Vancouver Groundcone | *Boschniakia hookeri* |
| Hooker's Fairybells | *Prosartes hookeri* |
| Baldhip Rose | *Rosa gymnocarpa* |
| Western Trumpet | *Lonicera ciliosa* |
| Trailing Blackberry | *Rubus ursinus* |
| Pathfinder | *Adenocaulon bicolor* |
| Red Huckleberry | *Vaccinium parvifolium* |
| Salal | *Gaultheria shallon* |
| Spiny Wood Fern | *Dryopteris expansa* |
| Spotted Coralroot | *Corallorhiza maculata* |
| Striped Coralroot | *Corallorhiza striata* |
| Thimbleberry | *Rubus parviflorus* |
| Tiger Lily | *Lilium columbianum* |
| Vanilla-leaf | *Achlys triphylla* |
| Wall Lettuce | *Lactuca muralis* (I) |

Fairy Slipper (above) and Vancouver Groundcone.

| Western Fescue | *Festuca occidentalis* |
|---|---|
| Western Flowering Dogwood | *Cornus nuttallii* |
| Mountain Sweet Cicely | *Osmorhiza berteroi* |
| False Lily-of-the-valley | *Maianthemum dilatatum* |
| Yerba Buena | *Clinopodium douglasii* |

**June:**

| Candystick | *Allotropa virgata* |
|---|---|
| Indian Pipe | *Monotropa uniflora* |
| Mock-orange | *Philadelphus lewisii* |
| Oceanspray | *Holodiscus discolor* |
| Three-leaved Foamflower | *Tiarella trifoliata* |
| Twinflower | *Linnaea borealis* |

## Western Redcedar – Sword Fern Forests

These forests occupy wetter locations than the Douglas-fir forest. Western Redcedar, Bigleaf Maple, Red Alder and Grand Fir are the dominant trees, with Sword Fern prevailing in the herb layer beneath. Many of the species you'll find in the Douglas-fir forest also occur here; so does Salmonberry, which is common in wet forests. Other species to find include Wild Ginger (*Asarum caudatum*), Stream Violet (*Viola glabella*), Wild Black Gooseberry (*Ribes divaricatum*) and Large-leaved Avens (*Geum macrophyllum*).

Western Redcedar.

Bigleaf Maple.

# Wet Forests

You may need waterproof footwear to explore a wet forest, except in the summer dry season. Two plant associations occur here. Cooley's Hedge-nettle (*Stachys chamissonis*) and Sitka Willow (*Salix sitchensis*) occur in both.

### Cottonwood/Crabapple Association:

| | |
|---|---|
| Black Cottonwood | *Populus balsamifera trichocarpa* |
| Common Snowberry | *Symphoricarpos albus* |
| Hardhack | *Spiraea douglasii* |
| Pacific Ninebark | *Physocarpus capitatus* |
| Nootka Rose | *Rosa nutkana* |
| Red-osier Dogwood | *Cornus stolonifera* |
| Scouring-rush | *Equisetum hyemale* |
| Slough Sedge | *Carex obnupta* |
| Pacific Crabapple | *Malus fusca* |

### Red Alder/Lady-fern Association:

| | |
|---|---|
| Giant Horsetail | *Equisetum telmateia* |
| Lady Fern | *Athyrium filix-femina* |
| Musk-flower | *Mimulus moschatus* |
| Palmate Coltsfoot | *Petasites frigidus palmatus* |
| Red Alder | *Alnus rubra* |
| Pacific Bleeding Heart | *Dicentra formosa* |
| Red Elderberry | *Sambucus racemosa* |

Stink Currant.

| | |
|---|---|
| Salmonberry | *Rubus spectabilis* |
| Stinging Nettle | *Urtica dioica* |
| Stink Currant | *Ribes bracteosum* |
| Fringecup | *Tellima grandiflora* |
| Western Redcedar | *Thuja plicata* |
| Skunk Cabbage | *Lysichiton americanum* |

## Wet Meadows

Wet meadows are open, unforested areas with moist to wet soils, including meadows, lake margins, ditches and similar habitats.

| | |
|---|---|
| Alaska Brome | *Bromus sitchensis* |
| American Speedwell | *Veronica beccabunga* |
| Idaho Blue-eyed-grass | *Sisyrinchium idahoense* |
| Bog St John's-wort | *Hypericum anagalloides* |
| Northern Water Horehound | *Lycopus uniflorus* |
| Field Mint | *Mentha arvensis* |
| Common Rush | *Juncus effusus* |
| Creeping Buttercup | *Ranunculus repens* (I) |
| Kneeling Angelica | *Angelica genuflexa* |
| Reed Canarygrass | *Phalaris arundinacea* (I) |
| Tufted Hairgrass | *Deschampsia cespitosa* |
| Tufted Loosestrife | *Lysimachia thyrsiflora* |

Skunk Cabbage.

Yellow Monkey-flower.

| | |
|---|---|
| Douglas' Water-hemlock | *Cicuta douglasii* |
| Pacific Water-parsley | *Oenanthe sarmentosa* |
| Hemlock Water-parsnip | *Sium suave* |
| American Winter Cress | *Barbarea orthoceras* |
| Yellow Monkey-flower | *Mimulus guttatus* |

# Lakes and Ponds

The lakes and ponds of the Victoria region owe their present form to the effects of glaciation, although some have felt some degree of modern, artificial control that has modified their volumes and submerged their original shorelines. Despite the changes, they offer interesting botanizing. Plants that grow in lakes and ponds belong to three groups: emergent plants growing on the edges are rooted in the mud beneath the water with their stalks and leaves emerging from the water; floating plants float completely on the surface with their roots taking nutrients from the water; and floating-leaved plants are rooted in the bottom mud with their leaves and flowers floating on the surface.

**Emergent plants:**

| | |
|---|---|
| Common Cattail | *Typha latifolia* |
| Emersed Bur-reed | *Sparganium emersum* |
| Soft-stemmed Bulrush, or Tule | *Schoenoplectus tabernaemontani* |
| Common Water Cress | *Rorippa nasturtium-aquaticum* |

**Floating plants:**
Common Duckweed          *Lemna minor*
**Floating-leaved plants:**
Greater Bladderwort      *Utricularia macrorhiza*
Floating-leaved Pondweed *Potamogeton natans*
Fragrant Waterlily       *Nymphaea odorata* (I)
Grass-leaved Pondweed    *Potamogeton gramineus*
Large-leaved Pondweed    *Potamogeton amplifolius*
Water Shield             *Brasenia schreberi*
Water Smartweed          *Persicaria amphibia*
Yellow Pond-lily         *Nuphar polysepala*

# Bogs

There were once at least six bogs on the Saanich Peninsula and more in the Langford area. Most were destroyed for agriculture long ago. The last remnant bogs around Victoria have been greatly impacted by hydrological changes in their catchment areas and have lost most of their characteristic flora. Good bogs, with their interesting plants, can be seen far afield from Victoria. One is at Jordan Meadows, southwest of Weeks Lake. Others are near Whisky Creek, Duncan, Ucluelet and Jordan River.

Apargidium                  *Microseris borealis*
Bog St John's-wort          *Hypericum anagalloides*
Buckbean                    *Menyanthes trifoliata*
Northern Water Horehound    *Lycopus uniflorus*
Crowberry                   *Empetrum nigrum*
Deer-cabbage                *Fauria crista-galli*
Three-way Sedge             *Dulichium arundinaceum*
Sticky False Asphodel       *Triantha glutinosa*
Northern Green Rein Orchid  *Platanthera aquilonis*
Hooded Ladies' Tresses      *Spiranthes romanzoffiana*
King Gentian                *Gentiana sceptrum*
Labrador Tea                *Rhododendron groenlandicum*
Lodgepole Pine              *Pinus contorta*
Marsh Cinquefoil            *Comarum palustre*
Marsh Speedwell             *Veronica scutellata*
Northern Starflower         *Trientalis europaea arctica*
Round-leaved Sundew         *Drosera rotundifolia*
Sitka Burnet                *Sanguisorba canadensis*
Spleenwort-leaved Goldthread *Coptis asplenifolia*
Bog Cranberry               *Oxycoccos oxycoccos*
Swamp Gentian               *Gentiana douglasiana*
Western Bog-laurel          *Kalmia microphylla*

Labrador Tea (top), Buckbean (right) and
Round-leaved Sundew.

# Coastal Beaches

These plants grow in the complex of habitats at coastal beach areas in this region, including sandy and gravelly beaches, tidal flats, salt marshes, and sand dunes.

| | |
|---|---|
| Seacoast Bulrush | *Bulboschoenus maritimus* |
| American Searocket | *Cakile edentula* |
| Baltic Rush | *Juncus balticus* |
| European Beachgrass | *Ammophila arenaria* |
| Puget Sound Gumweed | *Grindelia stricta* |
| Beach Bindweed | *Calystegia soldanella* |
| Beach Pea | *Lathyrus japonicus* |
| American Glehnia | *Glehnia littoralis leiocarpa* |
| Black Knotweed | *Polygonum paronychia* |
| Suksdorf's Mugwort | *Artemisia suksdorfii* |
| Beach Bluegrass | *Poa confinis* |
| Common Orache | *Atriplex patula* |
| Dune Wildrye | *Leymus mollis* |
| Giant Vetch | *Vicia nigricans gigantea* |
| American Glasswort | *Sarcocornia pacifica* |
| Seabeach Sandwort | *Honckenya peploides* |
| Barestem Desert-parsley | *Lomatium nudicaule* |
| Fleshy Jaumea | *Jaumea carnosa* |
| Lamb's-quarters | *Chenopodium album* (I) |
| Large-headed Sedge | *Carex macrocephala* |
| Meadow Barley | *Hordeum brachyantherum* |
| Canadian Sand-Spurry | *Spergularia canadensis* |
| Nuttall's Alkaligrass | *Puccinellia nuttalliana* |
| Pacific Alkaligrass | *Puccinellia nutkaensis* |
| Coast Silverweed | *Potentilla egedii* |
| Red Fescue | *Festuca rubra* |
| Salt Marsh Dodder | *Cuscuta salina* |
| Silver Burweed | *Ambrosia chamissonis* |
| Yellow Sand-verbena | *Abronia latifolia* |
| Sea-milkwort | *Glaux maritima* |
| Seashore Saltgrass | *Distichlis spicata* |
| Seaside Arrow-grass | *Triglochin maritima* |
| Sea Plantain | *Plantago maritima* |
| Thrift | *Armeria maritima* |

Salal.

# Coastal Western Hemlock Forests

The Western Hemlock forest depends on the heavy precipitation of Vancouver Island's west coast. From Victoria you will need to travel to East Sooke Park and beyond to find some of the zonal species.

**Forest**

| | |
|---|---|
| Alaskan Blueberry | *Vaccinium alaskaense* |
| Deer Fern | *Blechnum spicant* |
| Oval-leaved Blueberry | *Vaccinium ovalifolium* |
| Salal | *Gaultheria shallon* |
| Western Hemlock | *Tsuga heterophylla* |
| Western Redcedar | *Thuja plicata* |
| Sword Fern | *Polystichum munitum* |

**Alluvial flat**

| | |
|---|---|
| Devil's Club | *Oplopanax horridus* |
| Enchanter's-nightshade | *Circaea alpina* |
| Oak Fern | *Gymnocarpium dryopteris* |
| Coast Boykinia | *Boykinia occidentalis* |
| Stink Currant | *Ribes bracteosum* |
| Piggy-back Plant | *Tolmiea menziesii* |

# Conservation

The botany of our region is changing, and the main culprits are invasive species. No discussion about plants occurring here is complete without acknowledging the dramatic and devastating impacts of species that have been added to the regional flora, whether intentionally or by accident. Because there are now so many non-native species, the real difficulty is narrowing down the discussion to those having the greatest negative effect. Here are a few of the worst offenders.

No protected area is safe from the overwhelming effect of English Ivy (*Hedera helix*), literally and figuratively. This European ornamental has been spread far and wide and can now be considered among the greatest threats to parks in the Victoria region. English Ivy spreads easily, grows in both sun and shade, completely buries the native vegetation in the understorey, and then destroys trees by climbing up the trunks and making them vulnerable to windthrow. Volunteer groups spend hundreds of hours every year trying to remove this invasive weed from our parks, but it returns rapidly because it is so commonly found in gardens.

A more recent horticultural escapee that is fast becoming an enormous issue is Garlic Mustard (*Alliaria petiolata*). Not only is it tolerant of both sun and shade, but it kills other plants growing near it, making it a formidable problem for native ecosystems. Combined with copious seed production, it is definitely a major concern, and efforts to prevent its further spread are critical.

In open areas the two weedy species that most threaten the ecosystem are not popular in gardens, so there is some hope for getting these under control. The first is Scotch Broom (*Cytisus scoparius*), a leguminous species with a seed bank that can take 80 years to overcome! Spreading easily, shading out native wildflowers and changing the soil through its nitrogen-fixing activity, this species is having a significant impact on our Garry Oak woodlands. The second species is the Himalayan Blackberry (*Rubus armeniacus*). The difficulty here is removing it – it is well armed with thorns and it colonizes new areas readily by seeding through bird droppings.

Many species of grasses were intentionally introduced as forage crops for livestock, and these weedy species now occur throughout our region in greater abundances than any native grass species. For example, Reed Canarygrass (*Phalaris arundinacea*) surrounds many wetlands. This weed is difficult to eradicate, and in some protected areas it dominates the wetland habitat, choking waterways and affecting animals as well as other plants.

# Field Stops for Botanizing

## Victoria

Beacon Hill Park is largely given over to horticultural plants, but large specimens of the native Garry Oak and Douglas-fir are present. In less disturbed corners, remnants of the Garry Oak woodland and Douglas-fir forest vegetation can be seen. On the flats overlooking the waterfront, stands of Scotch broom and Gorse (*Ulex europaeus*) occur, as well as copses with Trembling Aspen (*Populus tremuloides*). Cow Parsnip (*Heracleum lanatum*) grows along the edges.

To reach Gonzales Hill, park near the weather observatory. A short walk along the road brings you to tiny Walbran Park and examples of grass balds and Garry Oak woodlands.

Anderson Hill Park is accessible via Island Road from Newport or McNeill avenue. A path leads onto the rocky summit of Anderson Hill. In spring enjoy the wildflowers of the grass balds and Garry Oak woodland. Look for hybrids of Western and California buttercups (*Ranunculus occidentalis* and *R. californicus*).

Uplands Park features a Garry Oak woodland and open rock outcrops. Park in the Cattle Point parking lot. Noteworthy plants in the spring are Macoun's Meadow-foam (*Limnanthes macounii*), found only on southern Vancouver Island, the not-so-common Straightbeak Buttercup (*R. orthorhynchus*), the Yellow Montane Violet (*Viola praemorsa*), Upright Chickweed (*Moenchia erecta*) and Tall Woolly-heads (*Psilocarphus elatior*).

Macoun's Meadow-foam.

The Swan Lake Christmas Hill Nature Sanctuary has parking at the nature house. The sanctuary has a small Douglas-fir forest, a wet meadow with Reed Canarygrass and a lake with Cat-tails and other aquatic plants. In moist areas look for Vancouver Island Beggarticks (*Bidens amplissima*), which is only found on Vancouver Island. Poison Hemlock (*Conium maculatum*) has been largely removed from the sanctuary, but persists in disturbed places in the surrounding neighbourhoods; it blooms in June. Also in June, another invasive weed, Salsify (*Tragopogon porrifolius*), displays its purple flowers along some city streets.

Bear's-foot Sanicle (*Sanicula arctopoides*) may still, rarely, be found in this area, on grassy flats and bluffs along the sea. It flowers from late March through May and has been previously found at Beacon Hill Park, Clover Point, Harling Point and Uplands Park. Look for it at Saxe Point.

## East Saanich

Mount Douglas Park has a parking lot near the summit. Enjoy the plants of a Garry Oak woodland, grass balds and the upper reaches of a Douglas-fir forest. This readily accessible mountaintop provides an opportunity to watch the parade of wildflowers throughout the spring, so start in February or March. You can also enjoy the plants of the Douglas-fir forest near the picnic area by the sea.

Island View Beach and Cordova Spit have a parking lot at the beach. Walk northward from the lot to the spit. Along the way you'll find sandy beaches, beach logs, marshy depressions and sand dunes. Look for Pacific Crabapple (*Malus fusca*) and Nootka Rose (*Rosa nutkana*) bordering the open areas. Then watch for most of the plants listed for the Coastal Beach Complex. On Cordova Spit, you'll find the Beach Morning Glory in June and Fleshy Jaumea throughout the summer. There are colonies of sand-binding Large-headed Sedge, American Glehnia and Yellow Sand-verbena. Gold Star (*Crocidium multicaule*) has also been found in sandy areas of Island View Beach.

Yellow Sand-verbena.

The summit area of Christmas Hill, just north of McKenzie Avenue, is part of the Swan Lake Christmas Hill Nature Sanctuary. Trails from the Swan Lake Nature House or from the residential areas north of McKenzie lead uphill to the summit area, which offers a beautiful sample of a grass bald and a Garry Oak woodland.

## North and West Saanich

Bear Hill Park is accessible from Central Saanich Road, Brookleigh Road or Bear Hill Road; the last takes you closest to the summit, with a short hike remaining. On top are tiny grass balds and Garry Oak woodlands. This is a good place to view spring wildflowers: Satin Flower in March, and later blue camas, Seablush (*Plectritis congesta*) and Yellow Montane Violet. Douglas-fir forest covers much of Bear Hill below the summit area. In May look for Spotted Coralroot (*Corallorhiza maculata*), Striped Coralroot (*C. striata*) and Tiger Lily (*Lilium columbianum*). In late June, Oceanspray (*Holodiscus discolor*) transforms the landscape to softness.

Elk/Beaver Lake Park offers great views from the water. Take a canoe out on these two lakes, now joined into one, to see the aquatic plants listed for Lakes and Ponds. At the lakeshore are plants of the wet forests. The park also has a fine Douglas-fir forest and large open fields. You'll find Cascara along the trail between Beaver and Elk Lakes.

John Dean Provincial Park straddles the summit of Mount Newton. Much of the mountain is covered by an interesting Douglas-fir forest; watch for Vanilla-leaf along the road to the summit. There is parking close to the top. The picnic area is a good place to view the impressive Western Trillium in April. Near the picnic area is a pond with Yellow Pond-lily and Common

Beaver Lake Retriever Ponds.

Seablush (above), Red-flowering Currant (right) and Vanilla Leaf (below).

Water Cress. Farther along the trail, also in April, you can see the humming-birds' favourite early spring blossoms, those of the Red-flowering Currant. At the south side of the summit you'll find a Garry Oak woodland and tiny grass balds.

Horth Hill Park can be reached from the Patricia Bay Highway (17). Go west on Wain Road, then north on Tatlow to reach the parking lot. From there it takes about 20 minutes to hike to the top. Enjoy the Douglas-fir forest and the wildflowers, and then the Garry Oak woodland with Arbutus higher up. In contrast, areas of Sword Fern and Western Redcedar occur along the south side of the hill, where underlying, tilted sandstone beds catch rainwater and keep the soils damp. In late April and May this area is resplendent with the blooms of Western Flowering Dogwood, British Columbia's floral emblem.

## Interurban Area

Thetis Lake Park is a plant lover's delight, especially in April and May, when its grass balds, Garry Oak woodlands and Douglas-fir forests come alive with spring wildflowers. Besides the plants listed for these habitats, this park provides a good opportunity to see the following, and more, noteworthy plants: Goldenback Fern (*Pentagramma triangularis*); Farewell-to-spring (*Clarkia amoena*); Naked Broomrape (*Orobanche uniflora*), a parasitic plant; Purple Sanicle (*Sanicula bipinnatifida*); Sierra Sanicle (*Sanicula graveolens*); Deltoid Balsamroot (*Balsamorhiza deltoidea*); Pinedrops (*Pterospora andromedea*), a parasite on mycorrhizal fungi, uncommon here; Howell's Violet (*Viola howellii*), in May-June; Dense Spike-primrose (*Epilobium densiflorum*); and Needle-leaved Navarretia (*Navarretia intertexta*) in moist meadows.

Thetis also has wet forests and lake species. Among its interesting aquatic vegetation is Wapato (*Sagittaria latifolia*) and Water Shield (*Brasenia schreberi*).

Francis King Park provides trails to view an interesting Douglas-fir forest, wet forests and a touch of Garry Oak woodland. You will see Slender Woolly-heads (*Psilocarphus tenellus*) and California-tea (*Rupertia physodes*).

Prospect Lake features the aquatic plants listed on pages 183-84. You'll also find California-tea by the roadsides in late June.

Naked Broomrape

Pacific Waterleaf.

## Highlands

The mountaintop in Mount Work Park can be reached by hiking up from Durrance Road or Munns Road. Enjoy the Douglas-fir forest with fine Arbutus stands and the spring wildflowers. In the western area of the park, be sure to visit the well-developed loop trails leading to McKenzie Bight in Gowlland Todd Provincial Park from Durrance Road (park just west of its junction with Willis Point Road).

In Goldstream Park, several hiking trails cut through Douglas-fir forests on the rocky mountainsides. Here you will find many of the plants listed for this zone, including Arbutus. The very keen may want to search out the Crinkle-awned Fescue (*Festuca subuliflora*). In the valley bottom near the mouth of the Goldstream River is a rich forest of large old Douglas-fir, Western Redcedar, Black Cottonwood, Bigleaf Maple and Grand Fir. Wild Ginger grows here.

A well-marked steep trail leads to Mount Finlayson from the Goldstream River, and is quite heavily used. The interesting south-facing grass bald through which the upper trail climbs is partly visible from the viewing area at the Goldstream Nature House. Across the picnic-area bridge, at the start of the Mount Finlayson Trail, grows Pacific Waterleaf (*Hydrophyllum tenuipes*). In April and May – sometimes much earlier – Gold Star (*Crocidium multicaule*) blooms in open areas on Mount Finlayson.

## West Shore

Mill Hill Park is approached from Atkins Road, which connects with Highway 1A near its junction with the Trans-Canada Highway. Spring wildflowers bring colour to the Douglas-fir and Garry Oak woodlands there. From February on you can find Hairy Manzanita (*Arctostaphylos columbiana*) in bloom, and California Comandra (*Comandra umbellata* var. *californica*) is present in late May.

Witty's Lagoon Park includes the beach, the lagoon and the rocky point to the east. Above the beach is a Douglas-fir forest and closer to shore are Arbutus trees and a copse of Trembling Aspen. Plants of the Coastal Beach Complex list are well-represented here.

Matheson Lake Regional Park, just off Rocky Point Road, has a lakeside trail that takes you through Douglas-fir and Arbutus woods. Look for Skunk Cabbage at the west end of the park. Western Redcedar dominates the damp area at Wildwood Creek and this stream leads out to a small marsh. Heavy summer use has severely damaged the vegetation and soils along the northeast shore of the lake. Gnome-plant (*Hemitomes congestum*), a parasite on mycorrhizal fungi, has been found in the park, possibly the nearest record to Victoria; look for it in July and August in areas of Salal.

## Sooke and Beyond

At Whiffin Spit, at the entrance to Sooke Harbour, you can see some of the coastal beach plants. Along the road to Port Renfrew, Douglas-fir forests gives way to rain forests. Places to view plants include East Sooke Regional Park (e.g., Skunk Cabbage near the Iron Mine Bay trail and Arbutus along the coast trail), French Beach Provincial Park, and China, Sombrio and Botanical beaches, all in Juan de Fuca Provincial Park.

Jordan Meadows.

195

Evergreen Huckleberry.

In forest areas look for the red and white flowers of Gummy Goose-berry (*Ribes lobbii*) in April, and the Evergreen Huckleberry (*Vaccinium ovatum*). The Nevada Marsh Fern (*Thelypteris nevadensis*) grows near the Sooke River Potholes Park – it has not been found elsewhere in BC.

Along the Shawnigan Lake-Port Renfrew Road you may see Vine Maple (*Acer circinatum*) and Pacific Rhododendron (*Rhododendron macrophyllum*). Both of these species are unusual on Vancouver Island, but common in other parts of the province. Jordan Meadows has interesting bog flora. It can be reached by a logging road running south from the Shawnigan Lake-Port Renfrew Road, about 9.5 km west of the Koksilah River canyon bridge.

# Reptiles and Amphibians

## Gavin Hanke

The Victoria region is home to 22 species of reptiles and amphibians – 17 native (though not all scientists agree that the Wandering Salamander is native to this region) and 5 alien. Amphibians and reptiles are among the most overlooked and disliked members of the natural community (along with spiders and slugs). While none of the species in our region are harmful, snakes are feared by many people and may be killed out of ignorance of the beneficial role that they play in our island's ecology. In contrast, turtles and frogs are nearly universally liked, even though the American Bullfrog, the Green Frog and the Red-eared Turtle are aliens and harmful additions to our aquatic ecosystems. In contrast to birds, flowers and butterflies, most reptiles and amphibians have secretive habits and tend to avoid humans. Naturalists must search to find reptiles and amphibians in the wild, and the pursuit is potentially far less productive than a day of bird watching. Most amphibians and reptiles go unseen unless you get very close, but then the startled animal races away – so, tread lightly and take only photos.

Pacific Chorus Frog.

Common Wall Lizard, introduced to Victoria in the 1970s.

The physiology and activity of reptiles and amphibians is governed by the environment, so naturalists should keep this in mind when planning a day out to search for them. Most reptiles derive heat from external sources such as warm rocks, road surfaces, or by basking in the sun, so it is usually worthwhile to search rock piles, debris, logs floating in lakes and sunny clearings for basking reptiles. The exception to this rule (in our area) is the endangered Leatherback Turtle, which because of its bulk and muscle activity, is able to maintain a higher body temperature than surrounding seawater. All of our terrestrial reptiles and freshwater turtles become torpid in cool weather and in winter, although the Common Wall Lizard may be active in winter in sunny weather. It is no surprise that you are less likely to find turtles, lizards and snakes on cool days or in rainy weather, but many of our amphibians are active in cooler weather, at night and after a rain-fall when the ground is uniformly cool and damp. Amphibians must keep their glandular skin cool and moist to breathe; so in the heat of summer, they may be found in ponds, lakes or streams, in shade, or under moss and woody debris.

Most of our local reptiles and amphibians hold few surprises to anyone familiar with the basics of biology, but three of our salamanders are lung-less (Family Plethodontidae). For some people, it may seem incredible that salamanders survive without lungs. Our lungless salamanders are small and absorb oxygen and expel carbon dioxide through their skin. They live and lay their eggs on land; they have to keep their skin damp, but will drown if trapped in water.

The Rough-skinned Newt, Long-toed Salamander, Northwestern Sala-mander, Western Toad and Pacific Chorus Frog are also terrestrial, but they return to water to breed. The Red-legged Frog, and both the introduced American Bullfrog and Green Frog are our only local amphibians that regu-larly inhabit aquatic environments as adults.

Long-toed Salamander.

The mating calls of frogs and toads are a sure sign of spring wherever you are in Canada, but do not expect to hear a deafening chorus of Red-legged Frogs each spring. Male Red-legged Frogs call from underwater and their annual courtship ritual is fairly quiet to land-based naturalists. The Pacific Chorus Frog is known to volcalize any time of year, but it is in the spring when their call is the characteristic 'ribbet' sound so commonly associated with frogs in children's literature and Hollywood films.

Our region's amphibians show an interesting variety of breeding behaviours and reproductive biology. Frogs, toads and the mole salamanders (Family Ambystomatidae) lay eggs in water, and their larvae develop as gill-breathing tadpoles in the manner familiar to most people. Some of our salamanders and the exotic Green Frog and American Bullfrog may over-winter as tadpoles and transform into air-breathing juveniles the following summer. American Bullfrog tadpoles have heads almost as large as a ping-pong ball, and may live two years or more before they transform to froglets and emerge onto land. In contrast, the eggs of our three lungless salaman-

Long-toed Salamander larva.

199

Northern Alligator Lizard.

ders are deposited in moist, sheltered places on land, and the young develop entirely inside the egg, hatching as perfectly formed, tiny versions of their parents. In their book, *Amphibians of Oregon, Washington and British Columbia*, Charlotte Corkran and Chris Thoms provide a handy key to help identify amphibian eggs and tadpoles in our region.

Local reptiles either retain eggs inside and give birth to young that burst out of a membranous sac (e.g., garter snakes and the Northern Alligator Lizard) or they lay leathery-shelled eggs in moist places where temperatures support the development of their young. Turtles are well-known for their nest-building skills, where they dig a flask-shaped pit, deposit their eggs and then bury them. Hatchling Western Painted Turtles overwinter in the nest, and dig themselves out the following spring. These hatchlings are vulnerable, especially when crossing roads. The exotic Red-eared Turtle has shown nesting behaviours in our region, but we are fortunate that no hatchlings have yet been found here. The presence of this exotic turtle in our region is maintained only by people contining to dump unwanted pets into ponds and lakes.

The exotic Common Wall Lizard can produce two clutches of eggs per summer. The females conceal their eggs under some sort of cover or in shallow burrows, and may even nest communally. The Sharp-tailed Snake also lays a few eggs in summer and they hatch in autumn. Once lizard, snake or turtle eggs start to develop, they will die if they are rolled, because the yolk smothers the developing embryo – if you discover a nest, do not disturb it because the eggs must remain in the same orientation to hatch successfully. Female garter snakes and Northern Alligator Lizards retain their eggs inside their body and bask in the sun to maintain the best temperature for the development of their young. Once born, their young disperse and live independent lives.

Most amphibians and reptiles are active on the surface from spring to fall, though their activity depends on the weather. Some amphibians remain active throughout the winter as long as temperatures are above freezing. Rough-skinned Newts, Long-toed Salamanders and Northwestern Salamanders can be found in mixed forests where lots of debris on the forest

Wandering Salamander.

floor provides shelter and a moist microclimate. These animals are easier to find in spring when they return to water to breed. Wandering Salamanders also live in coastal forests, in rotting logs, under loose bark and under clumps of moss, but unlike our other salamanders, they will climb trees. Wandering Salamanders are nocturnal and active in wet weather. Look for them in coastal Douglas-fir and Western Hemlock forests. Western Red-backed Salamanders and Ensatinas are found in moist areas under leaf litter, woody debris, logs, rocks and moss in our coastal forests. Look for any of our salamanders in lowland coastal forests where it is sufficiently damp, and don't be surprised if you find them under planters, pots or rain barrels in your own garden. Be careful moving large pots and barrels to avoid harming hidden animals.

Western Toads can be found in fields, forests, farmland, and a variety of marshes and other wetlands. When conditions are dry, they seek wetlands

Western Red-backed Salamander.

and moist habitat and may use burrows of other animals for shelter. Pacific Chorus Frogs are common in the Victoria region, sitting motionless in trees and other vegetation. They are fairly tolerant of human activity and can be found in most areas except densely populated urban places. In contrast, Red-legged Frogs inhabit streams, ponds, lakes and marshes at low elevation and may stray fairly far from water in damp forests, but are less tolerant of human activities. American Bullfrogs are found in Victoria as well as the surrounding ponds, lakes and marshes, and like the Green Frog, the distribution of these exotics is linked to human activity. Garden ponds may attract frogs, but more often than not in the Victoria region, it is the American Bullfrog that dominates a garden pond. Homeowners can support the ongoing efforts to remove this invasive species by eliminating all bullfrog tadpoles each autumn when you clean your pond, and by removing adult bullfrogs any time of year.

Our two lizard species are easiest to spot when they are basking on a sunny day, but sun-drenched lizards are fast, wary and hard to photograph. The Northern Alligator Lizard often is encountered in clearings and along rock outcrops with sun exposure, but they also burrow under woody debris and leaf litter in forests. The Common Wall Lizard frequents human habitation and disturbed areas. Alligator Lizards are silvery grey to copper-brown with large square-to-rectangular scales on the back, and tiny bead-like scales on the sides of the body. In contrast, Common Wall Lizards have a broad green patch on the back, and the scales on the back and sides are small and bead-like. Young wall lizards are coppery brown, with tiny scales on the back; young Alligator Lizards have small square-to-rectangular scales on the back.

Left: An unfortunate snake killed on a roadway. Right: Red-eared Turtles make the best of it after being abandoned by pet owners.

Western Painted Turtle.

Western, Northwestern and Puget Sound garter snakes live near water and are common in meadows, forests, coastal beaches, estuaries, marshes and lake shores. They can also be found in urban and rural gardens, where they do great service for gardeners as slug removers. Sharp-tailed Snakes are secretive, spending their time under cover of leaf litter, bark and rotten logs in clearings, forests and rural areas – even in compost piles. Urbanization of this region certainly has removed potential habitat for this snake. We know little of this snake's habits, so any sightings should be reported.

The Victoria area has been heavily impacted (to put it mildly) by human activity. Urban and rural development, from farms to houses to industrial and commercial centres, have eliminated most reptile and amphibian habitats that existed in the Victoria region. In recent years the pace of development has increased west of Victoria, with many houses, groomed lawns and gardens of exotic plants replacing natural habitat. Fortunately for our local flora and fauna, some refugia still exist, but these are becoming smaller and smaller islands of favourable habitat in the rising sea of urban development. Pacific Chorus Frogs are particularly successful despite our development of the region, and can be heard in many areas calling from trees in spring and after a rainfall. The exotic Common Wall Lizard is unique among our local reptiles in that it does best around human habitation and disturbed areas. It is not surprising that wall lizards are so abundant in north Saanich, where small farms and backyards provide ample habitat.

Besides human persecution, the biggest threats to reptiles and amphibians in urban settings are being flattened by motor vehicles and killed by Domestic Cats. Pet cats that are allowed to roam free outdoors kill countless snakes and lizards, as well as small birds and mammals – an enormous and completely unnecessary slaughter.

Western Painted Turtles inhabit slow moving streams, ponds and lakes with muddy bottoms and plenty of aquatic vegetation. Painted Turtles can still be found in Langford, Swan and Elk/Beaver lakes. Many of the other lakes in our region also count introduced Red-eared Turtles among their

An adult Sharp-tailed Snake can fit in your palm, while this young Western Toad can grow to be a handful.

residents. Beacon Hill Park and the Swan Lake Nature Centre are convenient places to see Red-eared Turtles released by ill-informed pet owners. These exotic turtles are also common on the Lower Mainland and some Gulf Islands.

Amphibians are an integral part of island ecology. Salamander and newt adults and tadpoles are carnivorous and take any bite-sized invertebrates they encounter. Our adult frogs and toads eat a wide variety of insects and spiders; larger frogs and Western Toads may eat other frogs, toads and small snakes, and American Bullfrogs will eat anything they can swallow, including small birds, shrews and rodents. Our local frog and toad tadpoles are vegetarian, but may also eat carrion if it is available.

Adult Western Painted Turtles and Red-eared Turtles are omnivores, eating a wide range of aquatic plants, freshwater fishes, tadpoles, frogs, salamanders, snails, aquatic insects and carrion. Young turtles are carnivorous. Leatherback Turtles eat sea jellies (jellyfish), a habit that gets them into trouble when they mistake plastic bags floating in the ocean for jellies and ingest them. Marine turtles are rare visitors to our waters and we do not know whether they feed here or how long individuals stay. Green Turtles and Olive Ridley Sea Turtles occasionally wash ashore dead or dying. Green Sea Turtles have even washed up at Esquimalt Lagoon.

Our two local lizards eat a variety of insects and spiders. Garter snakes in the Victoria region eat fish, frogs, salamanders, earthworms, slugs, leeches and tadpoles. Larger snakes can take hatchling birds and small rodents. The Puget Sound Garter Snake is the only local snake that routinely eats the Rough-skinned Newt, despite the newt's toxic skin, and the Western

Rough-skinned Newt.

Garter Snake is known to eat other snakes. The tiny, reclusive Sharp-tailed Snake feeds on slugs, and may use its tail to anchor itself while it subdues slimy sluggish snacks.

While amphibians and reptiles are important predators on small invertebrates, they also are food for a wide range of animals in our area. Our snakes and lizards can fall prey to gulls, crows, raptors, Raccoons and even American Bullfrogs, Green Frogs, Western Toads and large Red-legged Frogs. Local amphibians are prey for a wide variety of birds and mammals, as well as snakes and turtles. Local freshwater turtles have few predators, but I have seen Raccoons take adult Red-eared Turtles that were basking in the sun. Hatchling turtles and turtle eggs also are vulnerable to Raccoons, Mink, River Otters, Great Blue Herons, gulls and crows. There are even people on Vancouver Island who help eliminate bullfrogs by including frogs' legs as part of their regular diet (recipes for frogs' legs are available on the Internet if you care to try).

None of the native snakes in the Victoria region are venomous. Some people think that a local snake nicknamed the "Red Racer" is venomous, simply because it has a red dorsal stripe or belly; this marking is just a colour variation of the Northwestern Garter Snake, which is no more venomous that any other garter snake. It is safe to pick up any local snakes by the hand (their tiny teeth do little damage). But always keep in mind that exotic

"Red Racer" – a Northwestern Garter Snake with a red stripe.

A more typically
coloured Northwestern
Garter Snake.

snakes may be loose – some people in this province keep highly venomous snakes (even cobras) as pets, despite laws prohibiting such animals. Consult the Royal BC Museum handbook *Amphibians and Reptiles of British Columbia* to be sure you are familiar with all the species in the Victoria region.

When searching for reptiles and amphibians hiding under boards, logs, bark, rocks or any other object, remember to carefully replace everything as you found it to minimize the impact to the habitat. Both lizards on the island will release their tails if grabbed, and so lizard collection requires a bit more planning than simply charging up and grabbing the animal. The Ensatina also sheds its tail if molested, so be careful when handling this salamander. Turtles are easier to catch by canoe with a large dipnet. Once they slip off logs or rocks, turtles swim a short distance and re-surface, as if to try locate the intruder. If you can follow a turtle, you can get a net underneath as it re-surfaces. But remember, even pet turtles may bite, and while turtles lack teeth, their jaws can draw blood or leave you with a nasty bruise.

I catch frogs, toads, salamanders and newts with bare hands. The skin of amphibians is very sensitive, so *never* pick up any animals if you have put on insect repellent, hand lotion or sunscreen, or if you have just filled your gas tank or changed oil on a car or boat. Conversely, always wash your hands after touching amphibians and reptiles. The glands in the skin of Rough-skinned Newts produce tetrodotoxin (the same neurotoxin that is found in pufferfish); toads and salamanders also have toxic skin secretions that are not pleasant, and turtles are well-known for their ability to carry Salmonella. Before you go out to capture amphibians and reptiles, be sure to review the laws and be sure you can recognize all species that should be present. Permits are required to capture amphibians and reptiles even for short-term projects and never transport and release animals away from the capture site. You also need a permit to keep a local reptile or amphibian in captivity, even if only as a pet or for classroom observation; additional permits are required if you intend to work with species at risk (red- or blue-listed in British Columbia).

As of 2012, almost all of the amphibians and reptiles in our region are yellow listed and not of concern relative to the provincial wildlife ranking scheme, the Committee on the Status of Endangered Wildlife in Canada

Examples of suitable habitats for amphibians and reptiles in this region (clockwise from top left): the forested waterways of Goldstream Park; Matheson Lake; a sun-drenched rocky outcrop near Durrance Lake; an impounded section of Sandhill Creek in Central Saanich; farmland on the Saanich Peninsula; a backyard pond in Victoria; and a damp, shaded forest along Matheson Creek.

Northwestern Garter Snake.

(COSEWIC), and the *Species At Risk* Act. But their populations here are feeling the impacts of urban development. Some species are endangered already, and one – the Pacific Pond Turtle – is extirpated (locally extinct).

Pacific Pond Turtles were common as far north as Desolation Sound and were also said to be on Vancouver Island in the late 1800s. They presumably could have survived in the estuary of the Sooke River and in other water bodies along the east side of Vancouver Island. Pacific Pond Turtles have not been seen in British Columbia since 1966; their decline is attributed to overharvesting for meat. Where they exist today in the United States, habitat loss is the main threat to the survival of Pacific Pond Turtles, and in some places, American Bullfrogs are said to be significant predators on young turtles.

# Exotic Species

In 1950, the crew of HMS *Cayuga* found a Yellow-bellied Sea Snake (*Pelamis platurus*) in the ship's ballast water. This snake must have got into the boat when it was anchored or docked in Mexico. It is the only record of a true sea serpent in British Columbia. Fortunately, accidental importation of snakes to British Columbia is fairly rare and tropical sea snakes would not survive long in the cold waters of the North Pacific. But other exotic species present a growing threat to the ecology of our region and are recognized increasingly as a threat to global biodiversity. The exotic pet trade is a growing source of exotic reptiles and amphibians that can survive and even breed here on southern Vancouver Island.

Some exotic reptiles escape from confinement, but others (e.g., Common Wall Lizards, Red-eared Sliders, Yellowbelly Sliders and Common Snapping Turtles) have been intentionally (and illegally) set free. It is illegal to bring snapping turtles and softshell turtles into the province, and it is illegal to buy or sell Red-eared and Yellowbelly sliders in pet shops, regardless of whether the pet-shop staff claim that the turtles were bred in Canada. Unfortunately the laws are poorly enforced and pet shops continue to sell young turtles that grow until they become too big to keep, at which point the owners dump them into local waters. Red-eared and Yellowbelly sliders now live in warm, weedy lakes and ponds on the Lower Mainland, Vancouver Island and a few of the islands in the Strait of Georgia. Common Snapping Turtles have been released on Vancouver Island. These are powerful animals – do not underestimate the speed and reach of a snapping turtle's neck even though the turtle itself seems sluggish. You may not lose a finger, but the bite will be memorable.

The Yellow-bellied Sea Snake that arrived here from Mexico now resides in the Royal BC Museum's herpetological collection.

Most amphibians and reptiles in the pet trade are tropical, or at least prefer a warmer climate, but a fair range of North American and Eurasian species from temperate climates may survive here if released. Luckily, most pets are released or escape one by one, so the odds of breeding populations becoming established are slim. We are lucky that the Reeves Turtle (*Chinemys reevesi*), which was found in McCoy Lake near Port Alberni in the 1920s, either was a single individual, or if a few were released, they failed to establish a breeding population. A European Pond Turtle (*Emys orbicularis*) was also found on Vancouver Island, but again alone, and the species no longer exists here. In 2011, a wide range of exotic turtles were found

Yellowbelly Slider.

Large, hungry American Bullfrogs are having a negative impact on native wildlife.

in southwestern British Columbia, including a Spiny Softshell (*Apalone spinifera*) in Stanley Park, a Painted Turtle from eastern North America, a river cooter, more Yellowbelly Sliders, and another Reeve's Turtle. It seems that irresponsible pet owners are everywhere.

Of the exotic reptiles and amphibians that have gained a foothold here on Vancouver Island, the now-infamous American Bullfrog has received the majority of attention as an invader. Bullfrogs and Green Frogs were originally imported for food, but when the public demand for frogs' legs did not meet expectations and the production timeline was considered, the animals were released. They now have spread as far north as Coombs and Parksville on along the east side of Vancouver Island and also on the Lower Mainland to Hope. Bullfrogs exist in Washington and south along the Pacific coast at least to southern California thanks to many separate introductions. Green Frogs probably were a contaminant in shipments of American Bullfrogs because the two species look very similar and shipments were probably poorly sorted. A few Northern Leopard Frogs (*Rana pipiens*) also were found in Hamilton Swamp in the Parksville-Coombs area on Vancouver Island and were imported in the same failed attempts to establish a frog-leg industry in British Columbia. Frog tadpoles also are imported each year as contaminants in shipments of goldfish. In some cases, they are raised in aquariums or ponds and either escape or are released. While most pet owners mean well, they should never release captive amphibians and reptiles (or any pets for that matter) into the environment – the potential for disease transmission is great and the impacts of invasive species on the native fauna is difficult to predict. Once a reproducing population becomes established, it is extremely difficult to eliminate. It is far better to simply return an unwanted pet to a pet shop or find it a new owner.

In the late 1970s, a small group of Common Wall Lizards was released in Central Saanich. Initially, the lizards had difficulty finding mates, but once they acclimated they soon established a breeding population and multiplied quickly. These colourful lizards now number in the thousands and are starting to show up in other areas such as Commerce Circle (near Vanalman Avenue) in southwestern Saanich and as far south as Triangle Mountain in Metchosin. A few are said to reside a few blocks west of Hillside Mall in Victoria. Common Wall Lizards do best around human habitation and in disturbed areas. Early in their colonization of the Saanich Peninsula, they seemed to be restricted to buildings, rock walls and artificial structures, but they are becoming more common in grassy habitat.

The spread of these little lizards is accelerated by people who keep them as pets, or when lizards stow away in equipment that gets moved from place to place. Lizards in suburban areas probably arrive as eggs buried in the soil of potted plants. At the moment, we do not know whether Common Wall Lizards are having a negative impact on the native Northern Alligator Lizard in the Victoria region, nor do we have any estimate of their impact on our native invertebrates. Should these lizards accidentally or intentionally be released on the mainland, they have the potential to spread far south along the coast. This species of wall lizard was released in Cincinnati and has spread south to Kentucky and west to Indiana along the Ohio River.

We still have much to learn about the local reptiles and amphibians, and there is ample room for future studies. Naturalists can provide valuable data, observations of odd specimens and reports of rare or exotic species. Road-killed specimens, if in reasonable shape, can be sent to the Royal BC Museum. Public involvement is always welcome, especially if reports or specimens are accompanied by good photographs to help confirm identifications and detailed data on where and when animals were sighted or collected. The future of native plants and animals in the Victoria region is uncertain given the pace and magnitude of urban development, so it is important to document what exists here now in order to detect future changes, and set aside sufficient habitat to ensure that the unique flora and fauna of southern Vancouver Island is protected. Historically, amphibians and reptiles have been maligned because of miconceptions, but in this age of increasing education and widespread appreciation of science over mythology, perhaps people will appreciate these animals for what they really are: beautiful, fascinating, essential parts of our natural world.

Everyone can learn to appreciate the ecological benefits of amphibians and reptiles.

# Checklist and status of the amphibians and reptiles of the Victoria region.

| Common (Species) Name | COSEWIC | SARA | BC List |
|---|---|---|---|
| **Amphibians** | | | |
| Rough-skinned Newt (*Taricha granulosa*) | | | Yellow |
| Northwestern Salamander (*Ambystoma gracile*) | NAR | | Yellow |
| Long-toed Salamander (*Ambystoma macrodactylum*) | NAR | | Yellow |
| Wandering Salamander (*Aneides vagrans*) | | | Yellow |
| Ensatina (*Ensatina eschscholtzii*) | NAR | | Yellow |
| Western Red-backed Salamander (*Plethodon vehiculum*) | NAR | | Yellow |
| Western Toad (*Bufo boreas*) | SC | SC | Yellow |
| Pacific Chorus Frog (*Pseudacris regilla*) | | | Yellow |
| Red-legged Frog (*Rana aurora*) | SC | SC | Blue |
| American Bullfrog (*Rana catesbeiana*) | | | Exotic |
| Green Frog (*Rana clamitans*) | | | Exotic |
| **Reptiles** | | | |
| Northern Alligator Lizard (*Elgaria coerulea*) | NAR | | Yellow |
| Common Wall Lizard (*Podarcis muralis*) | | | Exotic |
| Pacific Gopher Snake (*Pituophis catenifer catenifer*) | XT | XT | Red |
| Western Terrestrial (*Thamnophis elegans vagrans*) | | | Yellow |
| Northwestern Garter Snake (*Thamnophis ordinoides*) | NAR | | Yellow |
| Puget Sound Garter Snake (*Thamnophis sirtalis pickeringii*) | | | Yellow |
| Sharptailed Snake (*Contia tenuis*) | E | END | Red |
| Pacific Pond Turtle (*Actinemys marmorata*) | XT | XT | Red |
| Yellowbelly Slider (*Trachemys scripta scripta*)* | | | Exotic |
| Red-eared Turtle (*Trachemys scripta elegans*)* | | | Exotic |
| Western Painted Turtle (*Chrysemys picta bellii*) | E | BE | Red |
| Common Snapping Turtle (*Chelydra serpentina*)* | | | Exotic |
| Leatherback Turtle (*Dermochelys coriacea*) | E | END | Red |
| Green Turtle (*Chelonia mydas*) | | | Accidental |

COSEWIC – Committee on the Status of Endangered Wildlife in Canada, www.cosewic.gc.ca.
COSEWIC ranks: XT – extirpated, E – endangered, T – threatened, SC – special concern,
NAR – not at risk.
SARA – Species at Risk Act, www.sararegistry.gc.ca/default_e.cfm
SARA ranks: XT – extirpated, END – endangered, SC – special concern, BE – being evaluated.
BC List ranks: Red – extirpated, endangered or threatened; Blue – special concern;
Yellow – apparently secure, not at risk; Exotic – moved beyond natural range
by human activity; Accidental – infrequent and unpredictable occurance in
our region.

# Additional Reading

The authors in this book have provided more extensive lists of references and additional reading specific to their chapters. You can see the latest updates of these lists on the Victoria Natural History Society's website: naturevictoria.bc.ca.

Acorn, J., and I. Sheldon. 2006. *Butterflies of British Columbia*. Edmonton: Lone Pine.

Arora, D., 1986. *Mushrooms Demystified.* Second edition. Berkeley: Ten Speed Press.

Brodo, I.M., S. Duran Sharnoff, and S. Sharnoff. 2001. *Lichens of North America*. New Haven: Yale University Press.

Cannings, R.A. 2002. *Introducing the Dragonflies of British Columbia and the Yukon*. Victoria: Royal BC Museum.

Cannings, R.A. 2008. *Birds of Southwestern British Columbia*. Victoria: Heritage House.

Cannings, R.J., and S.G Cannings. 2004. *British Columbia: A Natural History*. Vancouver: Douglas & McIntyre.

Corkran, C.C., and C. Thoms. 2006. *Amphibians of Oregon, Washington, and British Columbia*. Vancouver: Lone Pine.

Cresswell, G., D. Walker and T. Pusser. 2007. *Whales and Dolphins of the North American Pacific*. Madiera Park: Harbour Publishing.

Dombrowski, T. 2010. *Secret Beaches of Greater Victoria: View Royal to Sidney*. Victoria: Heritage House.

Druehl, L.D. 2000. *Pacific Seaweeds: A Guide to the Common Sea Weeds of the West Coast*. Madeira Park: Harbour Publishing.

Eder, T. 2001. *Whales and Other Marine Mammals of British Columbia and Alaska*. Edmonton: Lone Pine.

Eder, T., and D. Pattie. 2001. *Mammals of British Columbia*. Edmonton: Lone Pine.

Guppy, C.S., and J.H. Shepard. 2001. *Butterflies of British Columbia*. Vancouver: UBC Press.

Harbo, R.M. 1997. *Shells and Shellfish of the Pacific Northwest: A Field Guide*. Madeira Park: Harbour Publishing.

Harbo, R.M. 2011. *Whelks To Whales: Coastal Marine Life of The Pacific Northwest*. Second edition. Madeira Park: Harbour Publishing.

Hatler, D.F., D.W. Nagorsen and A.M. Beal. 2008. *Carnivores of British Columbia*. Royal BC Museum Handbook. Victoria: Royal BC Museum.

Jones, L.L.C., W.P. Leonard and D.H. Olson, editors. 2005. *Amphibians of the Pacific Northwest*. Seattle: Seattle Audubon Society.

Kendrick, B. 2010. *The Fifth Kingdom.* CD-ROM Version 5.6. Sidney: Mycologue Publications.

Kozloff, E.N. 1983. *Seashore Life of the Northern Pacific Coast: An Illustrated Guide to Northern California, Oregon, Washington and British Columbia.* Seattle: University of Washington Press.

Kozloff, E.N. 1988. *Plants and Animals of the Pacific Northwest.* Fifth edition. Seattle: University of Washington Press.

Lamb, A., and P. Edgell. 1986. *Coastal Fishes of the Pacific Northwest.* Madeira Park: Harbour Publishing.

Lamb, A., and B.P. Handby. 2005. *Marine Life of the Pacific Northwest.* Madeira Park: Harbour Publishing.

Lambert, P. 1997. *Sea Cucumbers of British Columbia, Southeast Alaska and Puget Sound.* Royal BC Museum Handbook. Vancouver: UBC Press.

Lambert, P. 2000. *Sea Stars of British Columbia, Southeast Alaska and Puget Sound.* Royal BC Museum Handbook. Vancouver: UBC Press.

Lambert, P., and W.C. Austin. 2007. *Brittle Stars, Sea Urchins and Feather Stars of British Columbia, Southeast Alaska and Puget Sound.* Royal BC Museum Handbook. Victoria: Royal BC Museum.

Lyons, C.P., and B. Merilees. 1995. *Trees, Shrubs and Flowers to Know in British Columbia and Washington.* Edmonton: Lone Pine.

Matsuda, B.M., D.M. Green and P.T. Gregory. 2006. *Amphibians and Reptiles of British Columbia.* Royal BC Museum Handbook. Victoria: Royal BC Museum.

McCune, B., and L. Geiser. 2000. *Macrolichens of the Pacific Northwest.* Second edition. Corvallis: Oregon State University Press.

Nagorsen, D.W. 1996. *Opossums, Shrews and Moles of British Columbia.* Royal BC Museum Handbook. Vancouver: UBC Press.

Nagorsen, D.W. 2005. *Rodents and Lagomorphs of British Columbia.* Royal BC Museum Handbook. Victoria: Royal BC Museum.

Nagorsen, D.W., and R.M. Brigham. 1993. *Bats of British Columbia.* Vancouver: UBC Press.

Paulson, D.R. 1999. *Dragonflies of Washington.* Seattle: Seattle Audubon Society.

Pojar, J., and A. Mackinnon. 1994. *Plants of the Pacific Northwest Coast: Washington, Oregon, British Columbia and Alaska.* Vancouver: Lone Pine.

Sept, J.D. 1999. *The Beachcomber's Guide to Seashore Life in the Pacific Northwest.* Madeira Park: Harbour Publishing.

Shackelton, D.M. 1999. *Hoofed Mammals of British Columbia.* Vancouver: UBC Press.

St John, A. 2002. *Reptiles of the Northwest, British Columbia to California.* Edmonton: Lone Pine.

Trudell, S., and J. Ammirati. 2009. *Mushrooms of the Pacific Northwest.* Portland: Timber Press.

Turner, M., and P. Gustafson. 2006. *Wildflowers of the Pacific Northwest.* Portland: Timber Press.

Wallace, S., and B. Gisborne. 2006. *Basking Sharks: the Slaughter of BC's Gentle Giants.* Vancouver: New Star Books.

Yorath, C.J. 2005. *Geology of Southern Vancouver Island* Revised Edition. Madeira Park: Harbour Publishing.

# Contributors

Dr Robert Cannings is curator of entomology at the Royal BC Museum (RBCM), where he has worked since 1980. He has written many books and articles on invertebrates, most of them on dragonflies and robber flies. He has participated in the work of the Committee on the Status of Endangered Wildlife in Canada (COSEWIC) by being a member of the Arthropod Subcommittee. Rob first joined the Victoria Natural History Society (VNHS) in 1985.

Claudia Copley has been the entomology collections manager at the RBCM since 2004. She has authored or co-authored several articles on insects, arachnids and other invertebrates. She's been a member of the VNHS since 1993. As a biologist and naturalist, Claudia spends as much time as possible exploring the natural world and is involved with many projects involving habitat rehabilitation and conservation.

Dr Anna Hall has a PhD in zoology from the University of British Columbia. She has worked for the National Oceanic and Atmospheric Administration and the David Suzuki Foundation, and she has authored and co-authored several papers on marine vertebrates. Her research has focussed on the natural history of local porpoises. Anna is a founding member of the British Columbia Marine Mammal Response Network.

Dr Gavin Hanke has been curator of vertebrate zoology at the RBCM since 2004. He specializes in marine and freshwater fishes, but has a keen interest in amphibians and reptiles. He has degrees in fish biology and biogeography from the University of Manitoba and a PhD in evolutionary biology from the University of Alberta. Gavin has been a member of the VNHS since 2005.

Dr Bryce Kendrick has studied fungi for more than 50 years and has authored over 300 mycological publications, including several books. He is an adjunct professor at the University of Victoria and a principal in Mycologue Publications and Consulting. Although best known as an authority on fungi, Bryce is a generalist, with a broad spectrum of interests, and he is deeply involved in the environmental movement. He first joined the VNHS in 2005.

Philip Lambert is curator emeritus in invertebrate zoology at the RBCM, where he was curator from 1973 to 2007. He has written numerous papers and three handbooks on the echinoderms (sea stars, sea cucumbers, brittle stars, sea urchins, etc.) of British Columbia. He's been a member of the VNHS since 1988 and is the organizer and host of the monthly Marine Nights, as well as an expert leader on intertidal field trips.

Alan MacLeod took up birding in Victoria in 1978 as relief from a career entirely unrelated to feathers or flight. Though strictly an amateur, he was for many years a birding obsessive, convinced life offered no finer distraction. After noticing a strong migration corridor over the southern tip of Vancouver Island, Alan was instrumental in the establishment of Rocky Point Bird Observatory. A member of VNHS since 1979, he has led numerous field trips and participates in several Christmas Bird Counts each year.

James Miskelly is a conservation biologist for the Department of National Defence, where he is responsible for the inventory and management of endangered species on military properties on southern Vancouver Island. He has participated in the work of COSEWIC by being a member of the Arthropod Subcommittee. James volunteers as a research associate at the RBCM and has been a member of the VNHS since 2003, where he coordinates the Society's monthly Butterfly Counts.

David Nagorsen was curator of mammals at the RBCM from 1982 to 2002 and is now a biological consultant based in the Victoria region and a departmental associate at the Centre of Biodiversity and Conservation Biology at the Royal Ontario Museum. His publications on mammals include numerous papers and several books, including handbooks on bats, lagomorphs, insectivores and rodents. Dave has been involved in conservation efforts through the work of the Terrestrial Mammals Specialist Group of COSEWIC and the Vancouver Island Marmot Recovery Team.

Ann Nightingale has been a member of the VNHS since 1997 and was president from 2003 to 2006. As coordinator of the Victoria Christmas Bird Counts since 2001, Ann is an integral part of the activities of the Society. She is also immersed in the work of the Rocky Point Bird Observatory, where she has served as president and co-president for many years. Ann often speaks at community events and writes for several birding websites.

Leon Pavlick (1939-2003) was a curator of botany at the RBCM for almost 20 years. An internationally renowned botanical expert, he wrote numerous books and was a contributor to *The Flora of North America North of Mexico*. He initiated the museum's "Grasses of British Columbia" project. Leon worked for BC Parks for several years as a naturalist and enjoyed writing about natural history topics.

David Stirling is a retired natural history specialist and tour leader who is widely respected for his knowledge of birds. While working for BC Parks, he spearheaded the creation of park naturalist positions. David is a past director of Nature Canada and the American Birding Association. He has written numerous papers, articles and books on nature, especially on birds. He's been the recipient of many awards including an honorary life membership in VNHS in 1995, the Queen's Jubilee Visit Medal in 2002, and the BC Field Ornithologists Award for ornithology in 2008.

# Credits and Copyright

## Text

Copyright for the Preface, Introduction and chapters resides with the authors, except for "Dragonflies", "Nearshore Fishes" and "Reptiles and Amphibians" © Royal BC Museum, and "Plants" © Royal BC Museum and Victoria Natural History Society.

## Photographs

Copyright resides with the photographer unless stated otherwise. All copyrighted photographs used with permission.  A = all photographs on the page; L = left; R = right; T = top; M = middle; B = bottom.

Terry Tuk: front cover, 6, 11.

Bruce Whittington: 13, 17, 29, 31L, 33B, 35A, 154, 155 (also on back cover).

Marie O'Shaughnessy: 14, 19, 23, 26A, 28, 31R, 34, 37, 39, 40, 46TL, 49BR, 50, 72, 115 (also on back cover), 123BR, 125T, 127, 138, 142, 144, 150A, 151, 153, 157.

Robin Robinson: 15, 30.

Glenn Bartley: 16, 22, 36L.

Daniel Donnecke: 20, 24, 32.

Mike Yip: 21, 27 (also on back cover), 33T.

Val George: 25, 36R, 44TR, 47L, 48, 177B, 193.

Jeremy Tatum: 43, 49T, 51.

James Miskelly: 44TL, 45 (also on back cover), 46TR, 46B, 47R, 49BL, 52.

Darren Copley: inside front cover, 44B, 54, 78, 82T, 93L, 123T, 123M, 135R, 140, 175A, 176, 177TL, 177ML, 177MR, 178, 179R, 183R, 189, 190, 192TR, 194, 196, 199T, 201T, 204L.

Barb McGrenere: 49M.

George Doerksen, © Royal BC Museum: 56, 58, 59, 60, 66R, 67, 69T, 69ML, 71, 72, 73A.

Robert A. Cannings and M. Brent Cooke, © Royal BC Museum: 57L

Robert A. Cannings: 57R, 66L, 69MR, 69B, 70T.

Derrick Ditchburn: 63L, 63R (also on back cover), 100TR, 106, 109, 111B.

Claudia Copley: 61, 65, 70B, 172, 219.

Royal BC Museum: 76, 209T.

Adolf Ceska: 80, 92T (also on back cover), 95M.

Bryce Kendrick: 81, 82B, 83, 85TR, 85ML, 85MR, 85BL, 85BR, 89, 90, 91, 92M, 92BL, 92BR, 95T, 95B, 96A, 98A, 104T, 171, 173, 177TR, 179L, 183L, 187.

Mary Hampson: 85TL.

Heather Wade: 86.

Paul Kroeger: 87.

Sharon Godkin: 93R.

Mike Beug: 97.

Philip Lambert: 99, 100MR, 102, 103, 104B, 105, 108T, 108ML, 108BL, 108BR, 111T, 114T (also on back cover), 169.

Pauline Davis: 100TL, 100B, 114B, back-cover fold.

Michael Harvey: 100ML, 108MR.

Angela Wyatt: 107, 113.

Tina Kelly: 112.

David Nagorsen: 117, 119, 128, 131, 132A, 135L, 136.

Steve Troletti: 120.

Ann Nightingale: 123BL, 185BL, 191.

Neil McIntosh: 125B.

Sherwood Patrick: 126.

"Mike" Michael L. Baird: 139.

Anna Hall: 141, 145, 146, 147, 149, 156.

Gavin Hanke: 159, 160, 161, 162A, 163, 164A (ML also on back cover), 165A, 167A, 168, 197, 198, 199B, 201B, 202A, 204R, 205A, 206, 207A, 208 (also on back cover), 209B, 210A.

Catherine Bell: 174.

Virginia Skilton: 180, 192B (also on back cover).

Thomas Ovanin: 181.

Nancy J. Turner and Robert D. Turner: 182.

US Canada Mission: 185T

Jason Hollinger: 185BR.

Bill Bouton: 192TL.

Dave Lynn: 195.

Michael McNall: 200.

Lyle Olsen: 203.

Laurel Neufeld: 211.

## Nature Guide to the Victoria Region

Edited, produced and typeset (in Plantin Std 10/12 and Optima 9/12) by Gerry Truscott, RBCM, with editorial assistance from Alex Van Tol.

Map on inside back cover by Rick Pawlas, © Royal BC Museum.

Cover design by Jenny McCleery, RBCM.

Index by Carol Hamill.

Printed in Canada by Kromar Printing.

East Sooke Park.

# Index

# Love Nature Too? Join Us!

**VICTORIA NATURAL**
**HISTORY SOCIETY**

The Victoria Natural History Society formed in 1944. It currently has about 750 members who have developed their interest in natural history in a wide variety of ways – some are professional biologists, others are students, most are amateur or volunteer naturalists, and many have taken up birding, botany or other natural history interests late in life. The Society provides an opportunity for those interested in the natural world to come together to share their ideas and experience.

The Society's primary objectives are to stimulate an active interest in natural history, to study and protect flora and fauna and their habitats, and to work with other societies and organizations with common interests.

The Victoria Natural History Society is a volunteer-run registered charity and non-profit society. It is a member organization of BC Nature (the Federation of British Columbia Naturalists) and it founded Habitat Acquisition Trust and the Rocky Point Bird Observatory to assist with habitat conservation and bird research in the region.

Four times a month from September to April the Society hosts evening presentations on natural history, birding, botany and marine life – all are free and open to the public. It also offers field trips for its members, ranging from weekly birding outings to summertime excursions. There is a wonderful variety of topics and destinations to suit every interest and ability.

Members receive the Society's magazine, *The Victoria Naturalist*, six times a year; they also become members of BC Nature and receive their quarterly magazine, *BCnature*. Both publications are filled with a terrific variety of nature- and conservation-themed articles. These magazines also publish project updates and publicize upcoming research and events.

To join or learn more about us, visit our website, naturevictoria.ca, or write to Victoria Natural History Society, PO Box 5220, Station B, Victoria, BC, V8R 6N4.

# ROYAL BC MUSEUM

British Columbia is a big land with a unique history. As the province's museum and archives, the Royal BC Museum captures British Columbia's story and shares it with the world. It does so by collecting, preserving and interpreting millions of artifacts, specimens and documents of provincial significance, and by producing publications, exhibitions and public programs that bring the past to life in exciting, innovative and personal ways. The Royal BC Museum helps to explain what it means to be British Columbian and to define the role this province plays in the world.

The Royal BC Museum administers a unique cultural precinct in the heart of British Columbia's capital city. This site incorporates the Royal BC Museum (est. 1886), the BC Archives (est. 1894), the Netherlands Centennial Carillon, Helmcken House, St Ann's Schoolhouse and Thunderbird Park, which is home to Wawaditła (Mungo Martin House).

Although its buildings are located in Victoria, the Royal BC Museum has a mandate to serve all citizens of the province, wherever they live. It meets this mandate by: conducting and supporting field research; lending artifacts, specimens and documents to other institutions; publishing books (like this one) about BC's history and environment; producing travelling exhibitions; delivering a variety of services by phone, fax, mail and e-mail; and providing a vast array of information on its website about all of its collections and holdings.

From its inception 125 years ago, the Royal BC Museum has been led by people who care passionately about this province and work to fulfil its mission to preserve and share the story of British Columbia.

To learn more about the Royal BC Museum, have a look at our website, www.royalbcmuseum.bc.ca, or write to us at 675 Belleville Street, Victoria, BC, V8W 9W2. Or, better yet, come and visit the museum in person.